Zen and the Art
of Information Security

VISIT US AT

www.syngress.com

Syngress is committed to publishing high-quality books for IT Professionals and delivering those books in media and formats that fit the demands of our customers. We are also committed to extending the utility of the book you purchase via additional materials available from our Web site.

SOLUTIONS WEB SITE
To register your book, visit www.syngress.com/solutions. Once registered, you can access our solutions@syngress.com Web pages. There you may find an assortment of value-added features such as free e-books related to the topic of this book, URLs of related Web sites, FAQs from the book, corrections, and any updates from the author(s).

ULTIMATE CDs
Our Ultimate CD product line offers our readers budget-conscious compilations of some of our best-selling backlist titles in Adobe PDF form. These CDs are the perfect way to extend your reference library on key topics pertaining to your area of expertise, including Cisco Engineering, Microsoft Windows System Administration, CyberCrime Investigation, Open Source Security, and Firewall Configuration, to name a few.

DOWNLOADABLE E-BOOKS
For readers who can't wait for hard copy, we offer most of our titles in downloadable Adobe PDF form. These e-books are often available weeks before hard copies, and are priced affordably.

SYNGRESS OUTLET
Our outlet store at syngress.com features overstocked, out-of-print, or slightly hurt books at significant savings.

SITE LICENSING
Syngress has a well-established program for site licensing our e-books onto servers in corporations, educational institutions, and large organizations. Contact us at sales@syngress.com for more information.

CUSTOM PUBLISHING
Many organizations welcome the ability to combine parts of multiple Syngress books, as well as their own content, into a single volume for their own internal use. Contact us at sales@syngress.com for more information.

SYNGRESS®

15116

Zen and the Art of Information Security

Ira Winkler

KEY	SERIAL NUMBER
001	HJIRTCV764
002	PO9873D5FG
003	829KM8NJH2
004	NBSD4298JL
005	CVPLQ6WQ23
006	VBP965T5T5
007	HJJJ863WD3E
008	2987GVTWMK
009	629MP5SDJT
010	IMWQ295T6T

PUBLISHED BY
Syngress Publishing, Inc.
800 Hingham Street
Rockland, MA 02370

Zen and the Art of Information Security

Printed in the United States of America
1 2 3 4 5 6 7 8 9 0

ISBN 10: 1-59749-168-3
ISBN 13: 978-1-59749-168-6

Publisher: Amorette Pedersen
Acquisitions Editor: Andrew Williams
Cover Designer: Michael Kavish

Page Layout and Art: Patricia Lupien
Indexer: Richard Carlson
Copy Editor: Judy Eby

For information on rights, translations, and bulk sales, contact Matt Pedersen, Commercial Sales Director and Rights, at Syngress Publishing; email m.pedersen@elsevier.com.

# Dedication

To the intelligence professionals in the field, who don't get the acknowledgement like the people in uniform, but are every bit as crucial and in as much, if not more, personal danger.

防Acknowledgments

First, I would like to thank Andrew (and not Andy) Williams, who was the only editor that would consider a project like this.   He is also the only editor that I was never tempted to commission a voodoo on. I can honestly say that this book is in the form that I envisioned it, and that is a major complement to Andrew. There are also many teachers I would like to thank, who related the subject at hand to more than just the subject at hand. These people are truly valuable teachers.

I unfortunately have to thank the people that make all of the security mistakes. Without their mistakes, I wouldn't have to write about the subject. More importantly, I want to thank the competent security managers and staff who have demonstrated how to properly handle security problems and implement security programs.

防Author

Ira Winkler, CISSP is President of the Internet Security Advisors Group. He is considered one of the world's most influential security professionals, and has been named a "Modern Day James Bond" by the media. He obtained this status by identifying common trends in the way information and computer systems are compromised. He did this by performing penetration tests and espionage simulations, where he physically and technically "broke into" some of the largest companies in the World and investigating crimes against them, and telling them how to cost effectively protect their information and computer infrastructure. He continues to perform these penetration tests, as well as assisting organizations in developing cost effective security programs. Ira also won the Hall of Fame award from the Information Systems Security Association.

Ira is also author of the riveting, entertaining, and educational book, *Spies Among Us*. He is also a regular contributor to ComputerWorld.com.

Mr. Winkler began his career at the National Security Agency, where he served as an Intelligence and Computer Systems Analyst. He moved onto support other US and overseas government military and intelligence agencies. After leaving government service, he went on to serve as President of the Internet Security Advisors Group and Director of Technology of the National Computer Security Association. He was also on the Graduate and Undergraduate faculties of the Johns Hopkins University and the University of Maryland.

Mr. Winkler has also written the book *Corporate Espionage*, which has been described as the bible of the Information Security field, and the bestselling *Through the Eyes of the Enemy*. Both books address the threats that companies face protecting their information. He has also written over 100 professional and trade articles. He has been featured and frequently appears on TV on every continent. He has also been featured in magazines and newspapers including Forbes, USA Today, Wall Street Journal, San Francisco Chronicle, Washington Post, Planet Internet, and Business 2.0.

Please visit **www.irawinkler.com** to learn more about Mr. Winkler and his work.

Contents

Introduction

Why You Shouldn't Buy This Book 1

Chapter 1

Zen and the Art of Cybersecurity 7
    Philosophy of Security 13

Chapter 2

Why I Don't Like the Title of This Book 15
    What Makes a Scientist 16
    Why Some People are Better Scientists 18
    Putting it All Together 22
    Applying Science 23

Chapter 3

What is Security? 25
    Risk 26
        Value 27
        Threat 29
        Vulnerability 31
        Countermeasures 34
        You Really Can't Counter Threat 35
    What is a Security Program? 36
    Optimizing Risk 37
    Consciously Accept Risk 41

Chapter 4

A Bad Question. 43
    Value has Nothing to do With Computers 45
    A Typical Security Budget 46

Determining A Security Budget 47
Multiyear Budgets 48
Remind the CIO the I means Information 48
Making Risk a Conscious Decision 49

Chapter 5

What Makes a Master 51
Mastering Computer Security 54
Taking Advantage of
Problems Built Into the Software 55
How Are These Bugs Found? 58
Fixing Software Security Vulnerabilities 59
Taking Advantage of How the
Computer is Configured or Maintained 59
Preventing the Configuration Vulnerabilities   61
Can you Master Information Security? 62

Chapter 6

Knights and Dragons 63
The FUD Factor 65
Dragons Forgive Incompetency 66
What If You're Not a Knight? 67
Terrorists Really Aren't That Good 67
The People You Really Have to Worry About 69
Real Computer Geniuses 69
Professionals 70
Opportunists 71
Script Kiddies 71
Look for Snakes, Not Dragons 72
Don't Suffer Death By 1,000 Cuts 72

Chapter 7

Cyberterrorism is Not Effective **75**
Anthrax vs. Nimda 77
It is Easier to Blow Things Up 78
What is a Terrorist? 79

Chapter 8

Common Sense and Common Knowledge **81**
Wanting Benefit Without the Associated Costs 83
Some People Are Just Stupid 85
The Wizard of Oz 87

Chapter 9

Never Underestimate
the Stupidity of a Criminal **91**
There is a Difference Between
Being Good and Being Effective 98
Understanding your Adversary 99
Insiders 100
MICE 101
Competitors 102
Foreign Intelligence Agencies 103
Organized Criminals 103
Criminals 104
Cybercriminals 104
Script Kiddies 105
The Criminal Mindset .106
Hiring Hackers 107
Your Kids are Notas Smart as You Think 109

Chapter 10

Information Security
Is INFORMATION Security 111

Chapter 11

Is Security a Should or a Must?. 115
Management Must Believe Security is a Must 119
So is Security a Should or a Must For You? 120

Chapter 12

If You Don't Remember History,
You Will Repeat It. 123

Chapter 13

Ira's Golden Rules. 129
Take Responsibility 130
Decide Security is a Must 131
Educate Yourself 132
Remember, You are Protecting Information 132
Protecting Your Computer 133
Use and Renew Anti-Virus Software 133
Use and Renew Personal Firewalls 134
Use and Renew Anti-Spyware 135
Run Weekly Backups 136
Use Uninterruptible Power Supplies 136
Note on Security Software 137
The 95/5 Rule 138

Chapter 14

Chance Favors the Prepared 139
Ubiquitous Security 140
The Purpose of This Book 141
Technology is Still Important 142

Security is Really Risk Management 142

Be Responsible 143

Appendix A

Critical Moments in Computer
Security History 145

Index 151

Introduction

Why You Shouldn't Buy This Book

This book is essentially one of the most well received and reviewed presentations that I have given around the world. I have delivered the presentation to ambassadors at the United Nations, business people around the world, academics at Oxford University and some groups of security professionals. Again, it is internationally very well received. I then realized that there are really no concise books describing security to any real-world audience, and began to move the presentation to book format.

The new format allows me to expand some of the concepts and deliver it consistently to a broader audience. However, it is essentially a set of critical security topics that don't usually flow together. The common bond is that they are very critical and basic security topics that are often overlooked or ignored. However, when you think about it, it is an ignorance of the security basics that allows for major attacks against computers and information as a whole.

With this in mind, I want to say that if you are looking for a book on Zen philosophy or Eastern religions, don't buy this book. The title is supposed to imply security philosophy, not religious philosophies. As I have written and lectured for well over a decade, good security is a good process, or set of good processes, not a technology. If people know how to approach security from a process perspective, the technologies are irrelevant. More importantly, great security is having a great security philosophy. Having a security philosophy means that your security processes will be well thought out, and most importantly, realistic. If you want to learn how to simplify security processes, and not be overwhelmed by the plethora of malicious threats you always read about, this is the right book for you.

Zen and the Art of Information Security intends to be unique. However, this book will not be all things to all people. I don't intend that there will be a lot of revisions to this book, as the content is not specific to current technology, and will be relevant for a long time to come. I was reading a review of my book, *Spies Among Us*, on Amazon.com and saw a comment that was intended to be a negative one about the book, saying that the book was not much different than one of my previous books, *Corporate Espionage*, that I wrote eight years before it. While the intended implication was negative, I thought of it as a huge compliment.

The reason that the review is a compliment is that it implies the content is timeless. The reviewer never said it wasn't a relevant book, just that there was relatively little new since my first book. It is true that *Spies Among Us* is essentially an update, with new title, of *Corporate Espionage*. While a book on Vista security may be critical when this book is initially released, eight years after the release of the Vista book it will be worthless, while this book will still be as valuable as the day it was released. Many readers at that point will not even know what Vista is. This book, just like *Spies Among Us* and *Corporate Espionage*, intends to be timeless as much as it can be. While technologies will come and go, the philosophies that go into implementing good security programs are timeless.

So if you are like the reviewer with tunnel vision, and are looking for a book that discusses securing the latest technology, don't buy this book. On the other hand, if you are looking for a book that describes how to approach security in unique and timeless ways, you should buy the book.

I fully recommend, however, that if you need to know about some specific technologies, you should buy books that cover those technologies. This book tells how to better take that information and apply it in real-world settings.

Similarly, if you are looking for a book that presents complicated discussions of the latest security issues, don't buy this book.

In my opinion, complicated discussions can bring up some interesting issues, but rarely will you be able to implement the material. More importantly, it doesn't help you take information that you might believe valuable, and allow you to easily transfer the knowledge to others who may or may not be as technically inclined as you.

This book simplifies the most complicated issues down to their fundamental principles. It is one of my hopes for this book that security people will feel comfortable giving it to as many people in their organizations as possible, which they can't do unless concepts are explained succinctly, clearly, and using language that the average person understands.

If you believe that the size of a book indicates its value, don't buy this book. Obviously, the book is "thin," and it is actually intended to be that way (much to the chagrin of my publisher that believes they could charge more for a larger book). Every chapter intends to leave you with a clear takeaway. The more concise the chapter and the more focused the content, the more you will be able to understand and begin to apply the key points of this book.

If you don't like analogies, definitely don't buy this book. I personally think that computer security has been plagued by people thinking that computers are some revolutionary product that has completely unique problems. There are so many lessons to learn from our every day experiences that can be directly applied to computer and information security. We are surrounded by so many other complicated but ubiquitous technologies, yet computer professionals have done an extremely poor job of pointing this out to others. This book makes very broad use of analogies to help people overcome their fear of what I believe are simple threats, but that the average person believes is some super evil entity that cannot be stopped.

I would normally say that if you are familiar with me and you don't like my previous books or writings, don't buy this book. However, I have come to realize that the people who dislike me the most are my most loyal readers. While I personally would not give my time to things that I don't like or that otherwise upset me, many people will devour what I write, spending days of their time trying to find any error, weakness, or any information that can be taken out of context. These people will micro analyze every word to try to look for something they can try to use to discredit or disparage me. So to those people, my most loyal readers, I say a sincere, "Thank you," and hope you find some enjoiment finding whatever problems you do. (Sorry guys. the misspelling is intentional for your benefit.) The second thing I would say to you is, "Get a life."

I really want all readers to first enjoy reading this book, and then to learn from it. And more importantly, to help you teach others this material. However, that also means that I don't want readers coming in with the idea that this book is an encyclopedia of security technology. Considering the page count, I really hope nobody thinks that. The fact again is that this book intends to address philosophies of implementing security and making it ubiquitous to business and life. This makes the book independent of specific technologies.

Admittedly, this book is small with regard to page count, but can be huge with helping you understand the true nature of making security a part of your daily activities. It is, however, not all things to all people. Hopefully though, if you approach this book with the right expectations, it can be one of the most valuable books you will read on the subject.

Chapter 1

Zen and the Art of Cybersecurity

I was on a telephone call that I avoided for weeks. We were planning how to steal $1,000,000,000, and to me this particular planning call was more than a nuisance. The instigator of the call is one of the most talented hackers I have ever met. Frankly, I would rate his technical skills as being among the best in the world. Yet, he was asking a bunch of questions about the pending theft that were not even worth talking about. Issues such as the timing for the specific phases of the theft, the hotels to stay at, and several others, were well established during previous calls and e-mails. However, he was going through the motions to make it seem like the most important question to him was just an afterthought.

After a few annoying minutes, he asked the question that he clearly knew the answer to, but he had to segue into the guts of his real question. "Who is doing the social engineering?" he asked with a purposefully naïve tone in his voice.

To the unexposed reader, social engineering is the hacker term for performing non-technical attacks. To most hackers, these attacks are typically pretext telephone calls where the hacker pretends to be someone to dupe an unsuspecting person out of information that can get the hacker access to a computer. Sometimes social engineering refers to going into offices and looking around for information about computer systems, such as passwords taped to monitors. That is the naïve view, in my opinion, of what social engineering is.

"It's going to be me, Stew, and Stan," I replied as a matter of fact, but in a tone that left no reason for doubt.

"What do we need them for?" he replied in an irritated tone.

"Well, obviously I am clearly the person to lead the work. Stew is a former Navy SEAL who specialized in infiltrating enemy positions to lay explosives. Stan is a former GRU colonel, who was one of their top spy masters and got people to betray their country under penalty of death," I replied in what I thought should be a definitive response.

Then my technical friend tried to metaphorically jump all over my statement. "Look, I know how to check for unlocked doors and look for sticky papers with passwords on them taped to monitors. We don't need to bring in any outsiders."

I have to admit that I was dumbfounded. This was not because he countered my argument so cleverly, but because I had what was an epiphany, for lack of a better term. The only thing that went through my mind was, "My God. You don't even know what you don't know."

Again, this was a person whom I considered one of the better hackers in the world, and who I would expect to know the difference between generic social engineering, the way a little Script Kiddie would perform it, and professional social engineering, which for all practical terms is human elicitation, a.k.a. spying. I would expect this person to realize that Navy SEALs undergo what is arguably the toughest training in the world because they have to complete the toughest missions in the world. Many people are not aware that the spy operations that people believe some James Bond would perform, are usually performed by Special Operations Forces.

Likewise, a real spy, like a GRU operative, completes years of training in manipulating people to get them to commit acts that are against everything they hold dear. It goes way beyond just asking for a password, which is frequently the word "password" itself. To a real spy, asking for a password and checking doors to see if they're locked is amateur hour.

For awhile, I tried to state how these people have years of special training that makes them uniquely qualified. However, social engineering can be the most fun task of any penetration. More importantly, it became a matter of pride for my hacker friend.

Nothing was going to change his mind. Luckily, when I wrote the targeting plan for the work, I put in the phrase "trained intelligence operatives." This made any other arguments moot as the hacker definitely did not attend any training by an intelligence agency.

As events would have it, Stan, the Russian spy, ended up identifying a possible Chinese Intelligence operation operating across the street from the company we were targeting. Stan walked into a Chinese restaurant and noticed a menu written in Chinese. He read the menu and noticed that there were Chinese delicacies on the menu.

"Ira, there are Black Duck Eggs on the menu," was Stan's confusing statement.

"Stan, what the hell are we paying you for? It's not to make me sick," I replied.

Stan laughed and said, "Oh my simple American friend. Black Duck Eggs are a delicacy in China. I can't get Black Duck Eggs in San Francisco, let alone this little piece of [garbage] town in the middle of nowhere. And by the way, they're cheaper here than on the streets of Beijing."

Then it started to click. Chinese intelligence operatives primarily work by recruiting people of Chinese heritage. To find as many potential people to recruit as possible, they create social situations where Chinese would want to gather. A restaurant, directly across the street from the headquarters of an extremely large global company, serving delicacies from home that cannot be found for thousands of miles, is the perfect situation to find people with access to the company and may also be more sympathetic to China than to the company. The intelligence officers just mingle with clients to find out who are those potentially sympathetic people.

There was no way in hell that my hacker friend would know how to read Chinese, let alone determine that the restaurant was a front operation for a major intelligence organization just by knowing that Black Duck Eggs are a Chinese delicacy. If this doesn't demonstrate the difference between the skills and knowledge base of hackers and trained intelligence operatives, nothing will.

I contacted the company's security manager and told him what we found and how to report it to the FBI. Oh, did I mention that this penetration was performed under contract for the targeted company to find their operational security vulnerabilities? The fact that we found an ongoing intelligence operation targeting the company was an added bonus.

While this whole case of a penetration test leading to the identification of a hostile intelligence operation is relatively unique, the concept that even highly skilled security professionals, like my hacker friend, not even realizing what they don't know is not. As a matter of fact, I contend that the major problem with computer security as a whole is that people in general are completely unaware of the basic issues of security. Again, as this case demonstrates, even experts in one aspect of information security may be naïve about many other aspects.

I realize that my hacker friend will be pretty upset about my talking about him in this way. While it is true that I believe he had a lack of knowledge in social engineering, the issue is that he was never exposed to what social engineering can be. If I was not directly exposed to human intelligence tactics, I would likely not know too much about the difference.

Frankly, I have worked with several security consulting managers at different companies, who all seem to take exception to the fact that I believe that trained intelligence and Special Forces operatives provide knowledge, skills, and abilities that even the best standard security consultants do not. They are as offended as my hacker friend.

It is not that I think less of people who don't have a special background, but that the operatives have years of highly specialized training that others do not. That training includes testing of implementing the skills in highly stressful life and death situations. Not only do they have the training, they have likely performed their work in real life and death circumstances. The average consultant who has not received this level of training and performed in the field just doesn't have anywhere near this skill level.

While it is true that the level of experience of the operatives is not typically necessary on a standard penetration, it is there when required. When you perform a penetration test, or espionage simulation in my case, 90 percent of the time it is so easy to compromise a company that a child could do it. Five percent of the remaining time, there is some situation that requires some additional skill that many skilled security consultants could perform. In the remaining 5 percent of the cases, the project will fail or be aborted without having that skill available.

However, while the above represents getting the basic work accomplished, it does not account for the fact that more than half of the time I perform the work, my team finds actual cases of criminal activity or espionage being performed against the client, like the case of the Chinese restaurant. Sadly, the clear majority of skilled consultants completely miss the crimes against the client. They don't know what they don't know about what they are missing. They can't find the activity, and they would not know the appropriate steps to take even if they did identify the crimes.

Philosophy of Security

Frankly, most of security is mental. How do you perceive what you are securing? How do you perceive the enemy? Do you believe the situation is manageable, or do you believe the situation is overwhelming? Are you willing to implement security into your daily operations? Do you consider security a ubiquitous part of overall operations? The list can go on.

How you answer these questions determines whether you will be secure. For example, a car is extremely complicated, probably more complicated than computers. Not only do you have to worry about the car itself, you have to worry about other drivers on the road, criminals who will vandalize or steal the car, failure of different components of the car, filling the car with gas, changing the oil, red lights, street signs, emergency vehicles, and so on. There is an infinite number of ways that you can be hurt either through your own actions or those of others. This could be very overwhelming, yet people get in their car every day and generally survive.

However, for some reason, people want to believe that computers are different. Despite the fact that scams have been going on in the real world for years, you would believe that scams were invented with the Internet. While it is not inconceivable that a savvy Internet user would be taken in by a scam, it is extremely rare. The only things that the savvy users have are common sense and some very basic knowledge.

Likewise, if you want to believe that computer hackers are invincible, you will do nothing in return to protect yourself. After all, why waste your money trying to stop someone you can't stop?

If you approach information and computer security like they are manageable, then they are. If you throw up your hands in defeat, you will be defeated. The way you think affects the way that you perceive and approach the problem. If you believe security is manageable, you will perform basic research, determine reasonable security measures, and implement those measures. I would say most importantly, you are taking personal responsibility for your security.

Once you understand the underlying principles of security, you can take reasonable security precautions. You don't have to have the training of a Navy SEAL or Russian spy to know how to protect yourself. This is true for both individuals and organizations, including multi-billion dollar corporations and large government agencies. If you understand why, the technologies and processes will follow. This book answers the Why of security.

Chapter 2

Why I Don't Like the
Title of This Book

Actually, I do like the title of this book. It is catchy. It also brings up connotations of the book, *Zen and The Art of Motorcycle Maintenance*, which gives the concept that there is a mental aspect to security. However, the title implies that security is an art. Security should be a science.

Art implies that there is no repeatable process. It implies that results can vary depending on the mental state of the practitioner. If something is an art, it cannot be truly learned. We then have to search for artists to do security work. We must then accept mediocre security professionals, because true artists are a rare commodity.

However, when something is a science, we can expect reliable results. We can find a variety of people to provide generally the same type of security architectures and services. Your company does not come to a halt when some people leave. Other people can then pick up where they left off, when they come onboard. Most importantly, if people are unskilled, you can train them to do an acceptable job.

What Makes a Scientist

When you find someone who is considered to be an artist, if you talk to them, you generally find that there is actually a science to what they do. If you ask them how a sculptor decides what to sculpt, they may initially say that they look at the rock and see what the rock tells them to sculpt. That clearly seems to be the method of an artist. If, however, you decide to question them on how they talk to the rock, you may find that the sculptor looks at the overall shape of the rock for clues. You may find that they prefer to sculpt certain types of objects. They may then look for inspiration in their surroundings or those of the areas around them.

Then they have their methods for chipping away the rock. They use specific tools and techniques. They use those tools and techniques in a repeatable method, which can actually be taught to others. While these artists may utilize a process unique to themselves, there is still a process to learn, understand, and apply.

Computer hackers like to think of themselves as artists. Again, however, the implication is clear that hacking a computer is a science and not an art. Let's specifically stick to the concept that hacking means breaking into a computer, and a hacker is someone who breaks into computers.

When I write articles, the ones that stir up the most emotions involve when I say that I can train a monkey to break into a computer in four hours. That comes straight from my argument that hacking is a repeatable process that requires little skill. However, self-proclaimed hackers hate this. The primary reason they commit hacking crimes is because they believe it makes them special. They believe that they have power and significance that others do not. When I claim that anyone with the time and inclination can do the same, it threatens their self-worth and self-perception of what makes them special in this world.

When you ask these self-proclaimed artists how they performed their supposed magic, much like the sculptors, they claim that there is something special about the way they do things that they cannot put into words. When you actually examine their actions step-by-step, you find that they actually have a process that they never defined, even to themselves. A typical hacker downloads a scanning tool from the Internet and then chooses a random Internet Protocol (IP) address range and sees what they get back. They look at the results to see if there are vulnerabilities that they have the tools or knowledge to exploit. They then use the tools or known techniques to break into the system and do what they want.

This is not the work of an artist, but the work of an amateur taking advantage of a computer left vulnerable by an unknowledgeable victim.

As implied previously, security is also a science. There are ways of systematically securing a computer, as there are ways of systematically compromising that security.

Why Some People are Better Scientists

If security and hacking, and any other science for that matter, are repeatable processes with predictable results, it is natural to ask why some people are apparently better at these sciences than others. The answer is that there are actually three interrelated factors that affect quality.

The first factor is the *training* of the process and maybe even the process itself. Clearly, some training is better than others. Some instructors are better than others. It is also a fact that some training programs are better for different types of people. Some people can grasp their training by only reading a book. Some people require hands on training, while others also need to know *why* so they can accept the importance of the *how*.

There is also the issue that some processes used in the security profession are just not very good. The training and/or processes being trained in are superficial, or sometimes too detailed, leaving students at a great disadvantage.

However, for the sake of argument, let's assume that most training and security processes are acceptable. With that in mind, another factor leading to expertise is natural *ability*. Different people have different abilities, and these abilities cause them to be better or worse in different fields of endeavor. For example, there have been thousands of professional basketball players. Clearly, people must be exceptional to make it to the pros. However,

Michael Jordan still sets himself up as an exceptional player among exceptional players. There is just some combination of innate abilities that he has.

In the computer world, there are clearly some innate abilities that allow some people to excel within the various computer fields. One such ability is known in the psychology field as visualization. One psychological test, known as VZ-2, more commonly known as the paper folding test, tests for visualization ability. This involves mentally manipulating shapes to determine what an unfolded object looks like after it has been folded. Figure 2.1 gives an example of this.

Figure 2.1

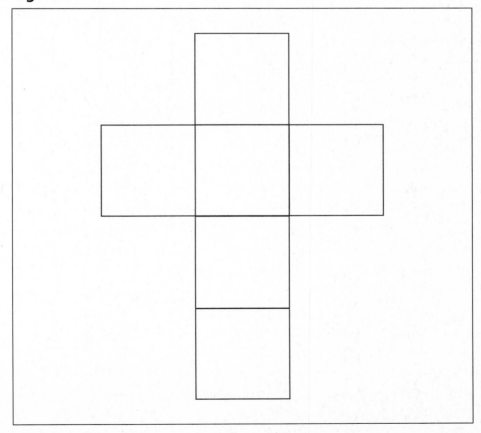

A quicker way of testing for visualization ability is to see if a person can point to the general direction of the entrance of a building as they sit inside it. If you assume that a person has walked into a building, turned right, left, or both, went up several floors, made more turns, and so on, if they can point in the general direction of the entrance, they have demonstrated that they can visualize the real world in their mind, and sequentially follow their steps. Whatever the reason, the better a person's visualization abilities, the better they tend to do in most computer-related tasks.

General intelligence is also an indication of possible success within any field. Probably more importantly, I think you have to consider the level of passion someone has for an endeavor. A person who loves the computer security field, or loves hacking for that matter, will be better or more effective at what they do. The rush that hackers get after they break into a computer leads to them being effective at specifically that, much like a junkie always finds a way to get their heroin. This passion is further addressed in the chapter on "What Makes a Master."

Additionally, some people have a passion that drives them to learn more about all aspects of computers. These people are not clueless script kiddies, but otherwise hard-core technical experts who want to learn as much about the details of computers as they do about breaking into them. The more someone knows about computers, the better they are at both breaking into computers and protecting them.

There are likely a variety of other mental processes involved in being an expert in the computer security field. Again though, a good training program can overcome a lack of natural ability to allow someone to be effective in the field.

The final factor that leads to expertise is *practice*. Any training that is not followed by real-world practice will soon be forgotten.

Likewise, natural abilities if not utilized will go to waste. There is no substitute for hands on practical experience.

Figure 2.2 shows the interaction between the three factors of expertise. The darker the color, the more likely someone is to be a real expert in what they do. I should point out, though, that it is impractical to believe that anyone has no training or no natural abilities. While your average script kiddie likely has no formal training, it can be almost guaranteed that they found information somewhere. There are hundreds of thousands of Web pages offering free information about how to break into a computer. They can find people at school and in chat sessions on the Internet to give them pointers on what to do. However, their "process" is generally raw and incomplete. It is a case where they have just enough information to make them dangerous.

Figure 2.2

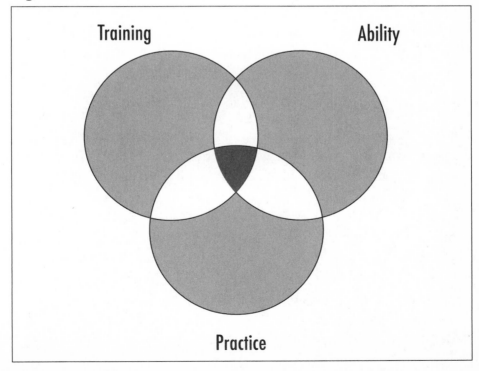

At the same time, it is extremely possible to get someone who has all the abilities as well as the training. Once that person receives enough practice, they are significantly better than anyone. There are plenty of people who fit this description.

Putting it All Together

Let me use Stan and Stew as examples. Again, Stan is the GRU spymaster and Stew is the Navy SEAL. Both of them were identified for having great aptitude in their skills. Both of them went through years of training before they received assignments in the field. Their training did not include just being a spy or saboteur.

Stew went through similar training as a Navy SEAL. After going through years of a grueling training program, which besides standard military training included language training, cultural training, as well as detailed information about a wide variety of potential targets. He performed a variety of operational assignments. Periodically, he was sent for training assignments. Needless to say, Stew has been very valuable in the espionage simulations that I perform.

Likewise, Stan received a variety of training in world history, Chinese and English languages, cultural information, and so on. He learned about the operational targets that he might be exposed to in the future. He was also trained as a journalist for his cover as a TASS reporter. He went through a variety of operational assignments, being given increasingly complicated assignments. Periodically, some assignments were back in Moscow for additional training.

So when Stan found the Chinese intelligence operation, was it just luck? He noticed Chinese-American dictionaries in our client's offices. Then knowing typical Chinese intelligence collection methods, he thought to check local Chinese restaurants for unusual activity. He was able to walk into the restaurant and read

Mandarin. Not only did he know the language, he recognized hard-to-find delicacies. He even knew what these delicacies should cost.

When I perform espionage simulations, is it luck that I consistently compromise the critical resources of an entire company within hours? The first time I took over a bank, it could have been luck. After the third bank in a row, it was clearly not luck.

The way I describe special forces and intelligence training is that people are trained to rapidly recognize vulnerabilities and then to know how to rapidly exploit them. While there is clearly some luck or chance in what vulnerabilities present themselves, eventually a vulnerability will present itself. Trained operatives recognize and exploit that vulnerability as it is presented. There is an old saying that is very applicable here: "Chance favors the prepared."

Applying Science

The question comes up as to why a hacker appears to have all this genius that computer security professionals do not. The fact of the matter is that law-abiding citizens do not go out and commit otherwise criminal acts. Given the mission, there are countless computer professionals who would accomplish the same, if not more, impressive results as just about any hacker out there. The media just likes to highlight the criminals, and as we will discuss later, anyone who knows one trick more than the general public seems to be a genius when it comes to computers.

For example, when the Department of Defense wanted to test their ability to detect and repel a cyberwar attack in exercises known as Eligible Receiver, they put together a Red Team of "hacking" experts from the National Security Agency and other elements of the Department of Defense. All of the individuals involved received their training through their various agencies and did not have criminal backgrounds. Yet, their results would have severely damaged many elements of the US civilian and military critical infrastructure if they fully executed their attacks.

Likewise, when I am putting together a penetration testing team, I look for people who worked for various intelligence agencies or military information warfare commands. Their training and hands on experience is unmatched. If I cannot put together a team of these people, I look for systems administrators who have successfully defended against hacker attacks for years. Either of these groups have demonstrated a deeper understanding of computer attack and prevention than any criminal could.

The most important thing to take away from this chapter is that anyone can be taught to do a competent job in securing their computer system, whether or not they are a janitor or a system administrator. Again, there is no magic to hacking or computer security. The issue is to make sure that the average person gets the basic training and that they practice what they learn. Just like the average person doesn't need to be an automotive engineer to drive a car, they don't have to be a computer security expert to adequately secure their computer.

What people need to do is understand that there is a fundamental process to securing a computer. Once they know what that process is, they can reasonably secure their own computers, whether or not they have any natural ability. All they have to do is implement and practice that process.

Chapter 3

What is Security?

There are lots of books about security, but few authors really know what they are writing about. The fact of the matter is that security is unattainable. You can never be secure.

According to the Dictionary.com, The American Heritage Dictionary, and the Random House Unabridged Dictionary, the primary definition of security is to the effect:

Freedom from risk or danger.

Your information will never be free of risk or danger. Anyone who tells you that they can provide you with perfect security is a fool or a liar.

Likewise corporate security programs are bound to fail, unless they really define their mission to their organization. Security is not about achieving freedom from risk. It is about the management of risk. Anyone who expects to achieve security will drive themselves crazy.

I meet many security professionals who love their jobs, but are living in a state of constant frustration. They don't realize that their job is to minimize resulting loss, not completely prevent loss.

So fundamentally, security is about the management of loss or risk. Information security is about the management of loss of information and the resulting cost of that loss, a.k.a risk. It is therefore important to define what risk is.

Risk

You can look up the word risk in a dictionary for yourself. It is more useful at this point to define a practical definition of risk. I prefer to use the following formula to express risk.

$$\text{Risk} = \left(\frac{\text{Threat x Vulnerability}}{\text{Countermeasures}} \right) \times \text{Value}$$

Risk itself is basically the potential loss resulting from the balance of threat, vulnerabilities, countermeasures, and value. Usually it is a monetary loss. Sometimes risk can be measured in lives. Sadly, many businesses put a value on human life to turn it into a monetary loss.

To quickly break down the components of risk, threats are the people or entities who can do you harm. Vulnerabilities are the weaknesses that allow the threat to exploit you. Countermeasures are the precautions you take. Value is the potential loss you can experience.

The following sections further discuss the components of risk at a high level. Again, this book only intends to provide readers with a functional knowledge of the subject matter. For a detailed discussion of this subject, please refer to my book, *Spies Among Us*.

Value

Value is the most important component of Risk. Without Value, there is no Risk. You technically have nothing to lose. Usually though, you have some value embedded in most things that you own or do.

Let's look at an example of value in something that might seem inconsequential. If you have a piece of paper with the location where you ate lunch yesterday, that would appear to be general worthless. However, let's say that you left your wallet at the restaurant. That piece of paper could then be worth a very large amount of money to you, or someone who finds the wallet.

Instead of leaving your wallet at the restaurant, let's assume that you were meeting a person you were having an affair with. The location of the restaurant could lead to divorce or blackmail.

If you are an executive for a large company, and you were meeting with people from another company that you were thinking of acquiring, or potentially were going to do business with, the location of the restaurant can help divulge the attendees and potential business relationship. If a competitor or even a person who buys and sells stock learned of a meeting, they could profit from the information.

On the other hand, nobody could care. As you see though, Value is a relative and fluid issue. As you can see by the above discussion, there are three different types of value: Monetary, Nuisance and Competitor Value.

Monetary Value is the actual financial worth of information or other assets. If you lose the asset, you lose money. This is a hard value. Sometimes it is difficult to put a hard value on something, but you can find a way to estimate it. If you don't, your insurance people will.

Nuisance Value is the potential cost of dealing with a loss. For example, while you may not have a financial loss related to an identity theft, the aggravation is priceless. For example, there is the time lost in dealing with cleaning up a credit report. While you might not be found liable for someone running up bills in your name, you have to take the time to prove that the bills are not yours. This process can take months of your time. Nuisance value must be considered in any calculation of Risk.

Competitor Value is the value of an asset in the eyes of an adversary. For example, credit card receipts are generally worthless to an individual after a transaction is completed. People usually take the receipt home and throw it out. However if the credit card receipt contains the full credit card number, it can be very valuable to a criminal.

A big example I give in the intelligence world is a marked up intelligence report. You can clearly not circulate a report that has been written all over and it is generally sent for destruction. However even a marked up version of a highly classified report can be extremely valuable to an adversary. It is no surprise that there is an intelligence discipline known as TRASHINT.

In the business world, a draft business proposal, for example, can be modified and worthless to the business itself. However if a competitor gets their hands on the draft, they can know almost exactly what they are competing against.

So while something might not have a value immediately to you, its Competitor Value means that it might cost you value in the future.

When assessing Risk, you first have to start with how much you have to loose. If you have nothing to loose, you don't have to worry about anything else. The reality though is that there is always something to loose, so you can't live in a dream world. However it is critical to know how much you have to loose to temper how much you spend on your security program.

Threat

The Threat is essentially the "Who" or "What" that can do you harm if given the opportunity. They cannot do you harm on their own. They require that you leave yourself vulnerable. Also, while people generally assume that Threats are malicious in nature, most threats that you face do not intend to cause you any harm.

First, you should consider that Threats can be either Malicious or Malignant. Malicious threats intend to do you harm. They include terrorist actions, malicious insiders, hackers, competitors, generic criminals, spies, foreign countries, etc. The type of harm the can cause you can vary by the type of intent they have. Again though, they have intent.

Malignant threats are threats which are always present. They do not have intent, however they have the possibility to cause you harm. Malignant threats are present in everyday life.

Unfortunately, the more you combat malicious threats, the more you enable malignant threats.

For example, I had a friend who died in a hotel fire. Basically, the fire alarm rang and she went running out of her room. The hall was too smoky and she attempted to get back in the room. However the lock on the door was one of those that automatically locked behind a person as they left the room. Clearly the intent of the lock was to prevent thieves by ensuring the doors locked as people left their room. However, this lock also prevented my friend from seeking shelter inside her room during the fire.

Likewise, there is also a major homeland security argument going on. The Department of Homeland Security wants to remove markings on train cars that indicate the type of poisonous materials inside the car. They believe that terrorists might specifically target rail cars with poisonous materials, like chlorine, as they enter large cities. However local fire departments need to know what is inside a rail car to know the potential dangers they face if a train catches fire, derails, etc. Clearly terrorists are a malicious threat, while fires and derailments are a malignant threat that actually happen quite frequently.

A *Who* Threat is a person or group of people. These are entities that can do you harm. They can be insiders who are either malicious in intent, or they just might be stupid employees. Threats can be competitors, foreign intelligence agencies, hackers, etc.

There are also many non-malicious people and groups that just exist, which don't intend to cause you harm, but do. These are malignancies. I already mentioned stupid employees. They can be your children. They can be Congresspeople passing laws that have a negative affect on a business. Vagrants can cause customers to feel unsafe, and therefore bypass a business. There are millions of people on the Internet who leave their computers vulnerable. While they may not want to attack your computer, their vulnerable computers can be taken over by a third party, who uses the computers to attack you. There are a seemingly infinite number of entities that may do you harm.

A *What* Threat is a occurrence such as a hurricane, earthquake, flood, snowstorm, etc. These threats are completely uncontrollable and agnostic in their intent. They do however cause more damage than any malignant threat could ever hope to. For example, Hurricane Katrina caused tens of billions of dollars in damage and the loss of thousands of lives. Power outages have a cumulative cost of billions of dollars as well, and are caused by a wide variety of natural disasters, or even something as simple as a tree limb falling down. Tornados seem like movie occurrences to many, but likewise cause the loss of billions of dollars and hundreds of lives a year.

When determine your risk, you have to determine which threats are relevant to your circumstances. Even though you might believe that you potentially face every threat in the world, the reality is that some threats are much more likely than others. As we will discuss in the next section on Vulnerabilities, the Threats are actually less of a factor than the Vulnerabilities that they compromise.

Vulnerability

Vulnerabilities are basically the weaknesses that allow the threat to exploit you. Again threats are entities. By themselves, they can cause you no harm. When there is a vulnerability for them to exploit, you then have risk. For example, let's say there is a hacker on the Internet. If you don't have a computer, there is no way for the hacker to exploit you.

Having a computer does present a low level vulnerability in and of itself. However, it doesn't have to be a major vulnerability. Consider of a person who has the user id of "kirk" and the password of "captain". That again is a very easy password to guess, so you are dramatically increasing the risk on the computer.

Similarly, there are many vulnerabilities in software, as further discussed in the chapter on What Makes a Master. The software itself, assuming it is not updated, is a vulnerability that can lead to a computer being compromised simply by being connected to the Internet.

There are four categories of Vulnerabilities: Technical, Physical, Operational, and Personnel. Technical vulnerabilities are problems specifically built into technology. All software has bugs of one form or another. A bug that creates information leakage or elevated privileges is a security vulnerability. Any technology implemented improperly can create a vulnerability that can be exploited.

Physical vulnerabilities are infamous. They range from unlocked doors to apathetic guards to computer passwords taped to monitors. These are vulnerabilities that provide for physical access to an asset of value.

Operational vulnerabilities are vulnerabilities that result from how an organization or person does business or otherwise fails to protect their assets. For example, websites can give away way too much. Stories about teenagers providing too much information on MySpace.com, which led to sexual assaults are commonplace. While people are quick to condemn teenagers, the US military currently finds that military personnel are putting sensitive information in their personal blogs.

Corporate public relations departments have released corporate secrets for marketing efforts. During the trial of Scooter

Libby, it was documented that Dick Cheney authorized leaks of classified information to try to discredit critics of the Administration's policies. These situations lead to critical losses, many of which the organization won't know about.

For example, when Libby disclosed that Valerie Plame worked for the CIA as an undercover operative, every country where she was stationed undercover went through their own files to see what cover companies she worked for. Those companies are now flagged as being CIA front companies. All people who ever worked for those companies are now identified as CIA operatives, and despite the fact that they are very well trained, they are now useless to the CIA. So while the apparent intent was to discredit Plame's husband, her career was ruined, as were the careers of dozens of other CIA employees. This is in addition to compromising probably over 100 past and ongoing intelligence operations that the dozens of operatives were involved in.

Personnel Vulnerabilities involve how an organization hires and fires people within organizations. It can also involve the contractors involved in the organization. For example, if a company does not check references, it is opening itself up to fraud. Likewise, if there are problem employees, a company needs to make sure that they identify the problems and treat it appropriately. For example, an organization that does not remove access for people who have left the company, those people can create future damage. While that might sound silly, there have been countless cases of where a fired employee was able to access company computers and steal information or sabotage their former employer.

Countermeasures

Countermeasures are the precautions that an organization takes to reduce risk. Theoretically, when you look at the Risk formula, the assumption is that a Countermeasure addresses a Threat or Vulnerability. You can decrease your Risk by decreasing Value, however that is outright foolish. Decreasing Value is a good way to get yourself fired. Ideally, you want to keep increasing your risk as the value of your organization grows. Likewise, it is probably better to have $1,000,000 dollars in a bank account that could be lost, instead of giving away all of the money so that you don't have anything to lose if someone hacks your bank.

Just like Vulnerability, there are the same four categories of Countermeasures: Technical, Physical, Operational, and Personnel. Technical countermeasures are generally synonymous with computer and network security controls. They include utilities like anti-virus software and hardware tokens that basically provide one-time passwords. These days there are thousands of software and hardware tools available as technical countermeasures.

Physical countermeasures provide physical security. These countermeasures include locks, fences, security guards, access badges, etc. Anything that stops a physical theft, or physically limits access to something of value, is a physical countermeasure.

Operational countermeasures are policies, procedures, and policies that are intended to mitigate the loss of value. This could include reviews of website content, policies as to what not to talk about outside of work spaces, data classification, etc. Any practice that intends to limit loss is an operational countermeasure.

Personnel countermeasures specifically mitigate the handling of how people are hired and fired. They include background checks, policies for removing computer access upon an employee resigning, policies to limit user access, etc.

It is important to state that technical countermeasures do not necessarily intend to mitigate technical vulnerabilities. Likewise for physical countermeasures and physical vulnerabilities, etc. For example, if you are concerned about passwords being taped to computer monitors, which is a physical vulnerability, a great countermeasure is a one time password token, which is a technical countermeasure.

You Really Can't Counter Threat

When you look at the Risk formula, it would appear that Countermeasures can address both Threats and Vulnerabilities. In theory, that is correct. In the real world, it is really difficult to counter Threat. The good news is that it doesn't really matter.

First, let's examine why you cannot counter Threat. Fundamentally, you cannot stop a hurricane, earthquake, flood, or other *What* threats. They will occur no matter what you do.

At the same time, you cannot really counter a *Who* threat. Maybe a background check can weed out known criminals, however this doesn't stop unknown criminals. While there is a War on Terror, there are still more than enough terrorists to create a terror threat. Maybe in theory, a government can attempt to hunt down a specific group of people to extinction, but a non-government organization clearly cannot. It is also unlikely that the government will succeed.

Again though, the good news is that you don't have to address the Threat. If you counter a Vulnerability, you are essentially countering any Threat that may exploit it. So if you recall the example of the password "captain" on the "kirk" account, by eliminating the "captain" password, you are eliminating the possibility that any malicious party may exploit that password.

With regard to a natural disaster, like a hurricane, while you cannot stop a hurricane, you can eliminate the vulnerabilities that lead to loss. For example, you can locate facilities outside of areas vulnerable to a hurricane. You can create backup facilities outside of hurricane vulnerable areas.

While you cannot stop a script kiddie from existing, you can counter the underlying computer vulnerabilities that allow the hacker to exploit you. Not only do you stop the script kiddie from exploiting you, you stop competitors, cybercriminals, malicious employees, and all other threats from exploiting known computer vulnerabilities.

What is a Security Program?

Now the Risk is fundamentally defined, I can address what security programs are supposed to do in theory. First, it is important to remember that you cannot stop all loss, if you function in the real world. No matter what you do, you must acknowledge that you will experience some type of loss. Actually, you will experience many types of loss.

In business terms, I would contend that the goal of a security program is to identify the Vulnerabilities that can be exploited by any of the Threats that you face. Once you identify those Vulnerabilities, you then associate the Value of the loss that is likely to result from the given Vulnerabilities.

The goal of a security program is then to choose and implement cost effective Countermeasures that mitigate the Vulnerabilities that will potentially lead to loss.

The previous paragraph is possibly the most important paragraph in the book for people involved in the security profession. Sadly I find that many professionals cannot succinctly and adequately state what their job function is in business terms.

Optimizing Risk

It is extremely important to point out that you are not trying to remove all risk. Again you can never be completely secure, and it is foolish to try. This is why your goal is to *optimize*, not minimize, risk.

Let's first discuss the concept of optimization versus minimization of risk. Minimization of risk implies that you want to remove as much risk, aka loss, as possible. Using a typical home as an example, first examine what there is to lose. Assuming you have the typical household goods, various insurance companies might say that a house has from $20,000-$50,000 worth of value, and the house has a value of $200,000. There is also the intangible value of the safety of your family and general wellbeing.

Then consider the potential things that could happen to compromise the home. Obviously, you have physical thefts. There is also the potential for a fire. There have actually been cases of a car crashing into a home. You can also not ignore that objects, including airplanes, have fallen onto homes, destroying them and all of their occupants. You have tornados, earthquakes, floods, etc. If you want to minimize risk, you must account for all possible losses, including some of the most bizarre ones.

Maybe if you are not in an earthquake prone area, you might think about ignoring that. However even if you want to just limit your countermeasures to account for theft, while you might think of improving locks on all doors, you then have to think of the windows. Are you going to make all glass shatterproof? Then consider that most homes are made of wood. There is technically nothing to stop a motivated thief from taking a chainsaw to the side of your house. Do you then armor plate the entire house?

So you can see that minimizing your risk, can lead to spending money on a lot of countermeasures that are not reasonable.

Maybe if you are the President of Iraq, you would consider all of these issues, but not the typical homeowner.

You can however not just broadly discount a great deal of risk. *Optimization* implies that there is some thought to the process. You don't completely ignore any threat or vulnerability, but make a conscious decision that the likelihood of a loss combined with the value of the loss cannot be cost effectively mitigated. So while it would generally be feasible to install a home alarm system for $300, and pay $25 per month for monitoring as a security countermeasure to protect $50,000 from theft, along with your personal wellbeing, it would generally not be cost effective to install armor around the home to protect against the extremely unlikely case of a criminal using a chainsaw to get in your house.

I like to use the following chart to represent risk, and to also clearly demonstrate why only a fool would try to minimize risk. The curve that begins in the upper left corner represents Vulnerabilities and the cost associated with them. The line that begins on the bottom left represents the cost of Countermeasures.

Figure 3.1

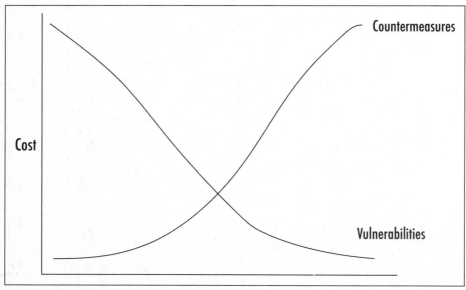

As you begin to implement Countermeasures, their cost goes up, however Vulnerabilities and potential loss decrease. Assuming you implement Countermeasures that actually address Vulnerabilities, there can actually be a drastic decrease potential loss. It is similar to the 80/20 Rule, where you solve 80% of the problems with 20% of the effort. I contend that in the security field, you can solve 95% of the problems with 5% of the effort.

Since you will never have not potential loss, the Vulnerability line never reaches 0 and is asymptotic. The potential cost of Countermeasures however can keep increases forever. So at some point, the cost of Countermeasures is more than the potential loss of the Vulnerabilities. It is illogical to ever spend more to prevent loss than the actual loss itself, so you never want to reach that point.

You also don't want to come close to that point either. The reason is that the potential loss is only POTENTIAL loss. While it is theoretically possible to experience a complete loss, it is extremely unlikely. You need to base the cost of countermeasures on the likelihood of the loss combined with the cost of the loss.

This is the concept of Risk Optimization and Figure 3.2 over-lays a sample Risk Optimization line on the initial graph. This is the point that you have determined is the amount of loss you are willing to accept and the cost of the Countermeasures that will get you to that point.

Figure 3.2

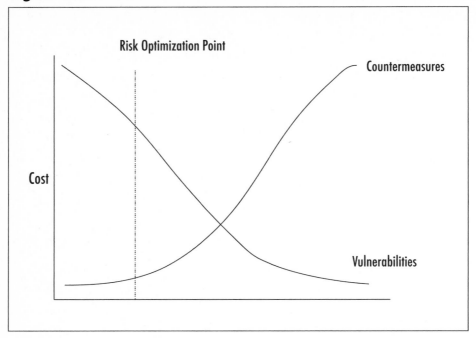

While I wish it was feasible to say that an entire security program should be based on this methodology, the reality is that most organizations are extremely far from implementing this on a macro level. Instead, I recommend that people approach Risk Optimization on a micro level.

For example, if you were to take a specific Vulnerability, such as bad passwords and determine the potential loss, you find that statistics show that it costs $40 per password reset. If you then determine that that a large organization might average one password reset per employee per year. For an organization with 10,000 people, that is a cost of $400,000 per year in just resetting forgotten passwords. This does no even address the loss resulting from the compromise of passwords which could be tens of millions of dollars a year in a large corporation.

If the cost of a Single Sign On tool or one time password token system costs approximately $1,000,000, and is good for 4 years, the average cost is $250,000 per year. You then consider that the Countermeasure is mitigating a hard cost of at least $400,000 per year as well as the loss of intellectual property totaling millions of dollars a year, the $250,000 is clearly cost effective.

A thorough vulnerability assessment can go through this process for all likely Vulnerabilities and Countermeasures.

Consciously Accept Risk

The big issue to consider is that Risk should be a result of careful deliberation. Whether you are deciding Risk for yourself or your organization, you need to realize that you it should be a consciously accepted fact. It is not a random result of a security program, but the basis for that security program.

If I were to ask you at this point in time, how much Risk do you face, would you have been able to answer accurately before reading this chapter? I also have to ask if you know that answer now that you have read it. If you don't, you really need to figure it out now.

Chapter 4

A Bad Question

There is an old saying that, "There is no such thing as a bad question." Normally I would agree with that. Unfortunately, though, some questions imply some fundamentally troubling beliefs that the fact that the question is asked is very bad.

The bad, yet common, question is, "How much of an information technology (IT) budget should go to IT security?"

The question is extremely simple, and would appear to have a very simple answer. It actually sounds very logical. Unfortunately, though, the people asking the question are demonstrating no understanding of business concepts.

Let me first ask you what percentage of a building's costs should be allocated to security? How would you reply to me? Would you ask me what type of building it is? Is it an empty warehouse? Is it a bank? Is it a military outpost in downtown Baghdad?

You have to consider the value of what's inside the building long before you consider what percent of a building's budget should go to security. All three potential buildings described might cost the same to construct. However, the cost of the security of the military outpost might well exceed the construction costs. You likewise might spend nothing on securing an empty building.

This chapter was originally included in the previous chapter. However, I believe that this concept is so important it must be highlighted. Too many security programs are fundamentally flawed because of the thought that a budget can produce security.

Value has Nothing to do With Computers

So, with the example of the buildings in mind, how would you answer the question about the percentage of an IT budget that should go to security? You might first ask, what is the use of the IT?

A bank may have a $100,000,000 IT budget, but the reality is that the bank is protecting the billions of dollars of transactions that go through the bank's computers each day. The actual cost of the IT budget is irrelevant.

Look at that mathematically. Let's be generous and say that the bank would allocate 10 percent of their IT budget to security. That's $10,000,000 annually; a number many security managers would be thrilled with. Then if you assume that there are 250 business days per year and the bank does minimally $1,000,000,000 daily of financial transactions. The bank is therefore protecting $250,000,000,000 with $10,000,000. That is actually a security budget of .004 percent of the actual value being protected.

The situation is similar for pharmaceutical companies that may have a reasonable security budget, but the value of the intellectual property on the computers is worth billions of dollars. There are clearly other industries where the value of the information is well above the value of the IT.

You must also consider the issue that security is not just an IT issue. As previously discussed in the last chapter, technology can be compromised through other than technical means. You cannot protect IT solely through the use of IT Countermeasures. Physical Countermeasures have to be considered in the mix. Similarly, you need to incorporate Operational and Personnel Countermeasures. You cannot just say that you are protecting IT as an IT issue.

Another issue to consider is the current state of security of an organization. If you think back to the example of the buildings, if a building already has bulletproof glass, thick walls, perimeter fences, etc., you don't need to budget for those countermeasures. Likewise, if your IT infrastructure is already embedded with security countermeasures, you don't need to purchase them new. You don't need to pay for installing them. You don't need to send your entire staff for training. So an organization that has a fundamentally secure IT infrastructure can generally devote less funding to their budget for security.

A Typical Security Budget

Security budgets are typically assigned to the security managers. As sadly stated, most of the time the IT security budget is a specific percentage of the IT budget. It is frequently not integrated with the budget of other security departments. The IT security manager must then choose the countermeasures to implement based on that budget.

Frequently, a security manager requests a larger budget, because they want to implement specific Countermeasures. The logic that they use is that the Countermeasures are needed. Unfortunately these well meaning people never provide a true financial justification, just a presentation of intuition. It is not that I believe the intuition is wrong; just that it is not presented in a way management can easily justify.

In this case, the resulting Risk is completely random. The IT security manager will typically spend a large portion of their budget on "staples" such as anti-virus software, firewalls, annual assessments, etc. In many companies, a large portion of the budget is allocated to compliance testing required by law, such as HIPAA and SOX compliance.

This generally does not leave much money for making improvements. The only hope many security managers have to get new Countermeasures implemented is for the auditors performing the compliance testing to state that the Countermeasures are required to pass the tests. Again, there is no proactive consideration to the resulting loss an organization may experience.

Determining A Security Budget

The reason that a well secured organization needs a smaller security budget is because they have already implemented many Countermeasures and have fewer Vulnerabilities. It is that simple. You may have to pay to maintain the Countermeasures, but that is usually less expensive than buying or initially implementing the Countermeasures.

The steps then to determine a security budget is to do the following:

1. Determine the Vulnerabilities that exist
2. Determine the probably loss from each of those Vulnerabilities
3. Determine the Countermeasures that can mitigate the Vulnerabilities
4. Determine the cost of the Countermeasures
5. Determine whether a Countermeasure can mitigate more than one Vulnerability
6. Choose the Countermeasures that have a clear return on investment (ROI)
7. Calculate the budget required for those countermeasures

This financially justified methodology for determining security budgets. If management chooses not to fund a recommended Countermeasure, you can then tell them that their failure to approve \$X in the budget will likely create \$Y of loss. It is putting the hones on management, who has made a conscious decision to ignore your advice.

Multiyear Budgets

Sometimes it is not financially or logistically feasible to implement all desired Countermeasures within a single year. In this case, you need to figure out the ideal state and the likely time period it will take to get it to that state. At that point, you can then figure out the yearly budget for all the desired Countermeasures.

Remind the CIO the I means Information

Frequently senior management has a hard time taking a security person seriously when they start talking in business terms. The fact of the matter is that the Chief Information Officer is a relatively new position in the business world. Previously, the most senior IT professional was a Vice President or Director of IT, who usually reported to the Chief Financial Officer. This was known as the concept of the Management of Information Systems.

In the late 1980s, businesses began to adopt the concept of Information Resources Management (IRM). This is the fundamental concept that the true value of computer systems is the information or services that the computers provide. Since information was as valuable as money to organizations, the person in charge of computer systems was elevated in stature to a C level position. Again, it is the information and not computer systems that is perceived to have value.

Unfortunately, the whole security mindset that I describe, about security efforts being given random budgets, is with the

Management of Information Systems mindset. Security hasn't caught up to IRM principles.

So, if you meet resistance in implementing the Risk methodology that I describe, you should remind the CIO that his title is not Chief Computer Officer, but Chief Information Officer.

Making Risk a Conscious Decision

There are many ways you can spend money when it comes to security. If you choose to spend money that you are randomly allocated, then you are randomly ruining your safety. It is not easy to purposefully assess Risk either for yourself or your business.

Then again, nobody says that things are supposed to be easy. Frankly, either way it seems that you have a hard job. If you don't try to purposefully calculate Risk, you will definitely have a lot to handle, because incidents will happen all over the place. If you do go through the trouble and calculate Risk, you will likely have much more control when incidents do occur and the loss will be minimized.

When you can present management with a clear idea of the costs and benefits associated with your budget requests, you are making Risk a conscious decision for yourself and your organization.

Chapter 5

What Makes
a Master

I have studied several forms of martial arts, achieving varying levels of expertise in each. While most people believe that black belts or martial arts masters know some special, mysterious skills that require years of dedication to attain, the more I studied, the more I realized that there was no secret.

The fact of the matter is that there are only so many ways to punch, kick, and block. A *master*, by definition, is someone who has *mastered* something. To master anything, it takes a combination of learning basic skills and perfecting those skills through practice. In the martial arts, a master has learned and perfected the basics of punching, kicking, and blocking. For example, a master has practiced his art to learn how to punch with power, and where to punch to maximize its effectiveness. They have practiced against many different types of opponents, so they know how to apply their techniques best against different body types and fighting styles. The master can then combine basics in ways that look mystical.

As you perfect some skills, you can learn others. Fundamentally though, there is little difference in the knowledge base of a white belt compared to a black belt. The black belt has had significantly more practice and knowledge in applying the fundamentals.

A black belt, however, is not necessarily a master. There are many black belts who are actually barely competent. They learn enough to pass tests, and may even look very impressive to the non-practitioners. However, they have not devoted the time to practicing, developing, and refining their skills like the masters have, or even like a devoted martial artist.

Likewise, there are "Master" levels in a variety of other endeavors. For example, I am also a Dive Master. While I clearly had to learn some specific issues about leading dives and dive safety, the bulk of the criteria involved in obtaining a Dive Master rating involved demonstrating a mastery of 20 basic diving skills. There are similar master ratings in professional fields like plumbing.

Once you identify the basics that people must learn to be designated a Master in their given endeavor, anyone can learn to be a master assuming that they have the dedication to practice and perfect those basics. Clearly, those basics must be clearly defined, and receiving tutoring or other assistance can help the process along. I must say that this does sound easier than it actually is, and that is actually a good thing.

I did specifically state that someone needs dedication to practice. Of course, many people want to become Masters. The reality, though, is that they don't want to put the required work into the practice and studying of mastering the required basics. Without a passion and discipline for the chosen endeavor, it is not likely that a person will master it.

However, just because you are not a master in a field, it doesn't mean that you cannot perform competently in that field. For example, while there are relatively few Dive Masters, tens of millions of people have safely scuba dove around the world. They have an acceptable understanding of basic dive safety and skills, and can use those skills in the real world.

Similarly, you don't have to be a Master Plumber to competently fix a leaky faucet; you just need a basic understanding of the mechanics of the faucet and the right equipment.

Likewise, it is very important to realize that just because you can fix a faucet, it does not make you a Master Plumber. Just because you can dive safely, it doesn't make you a Dive Master. While you can apply basic skills, a master has a broader set of skills and can apply the broad set of skills under a broad set of circumstances. So, for example, just because you may be able to fix a leaky toilet, it doesn't mean you are capable of designing the plumbing for a high-rise building.

Another clear skill a true master has is that they understand the limits of their mastery. For example, an American Kenpo Karate Master is not going to claim to be an expert in Kung Fu. For that matter, the American Kenpo Karate Master will not claim to be a master in Chinese Kenpo. However, the American Kenpo Master will likely have studied the basics of the other arts to potentially study how to apply their techniques against the other arts, and to refine their art with components of the other arts they study.

Ironically, though, the person I spoke about in the first chapter, who was truly a master in "computer hacking," who thought that checking doors to see if they're locked was all that was needed for social engineering, did not appreciate the concepts of the other arts composing the broad field of Information Security. Sadly, I believe his or her mastery of computer security will be limited, because he or she doesn't understand or appreciate the expertise required in human intelligence, so he or she will not spend time studying how to improve his skills in that area. Nor will he or she be able to fully appreciate the components that need to go into a security awareness program to address well-trained people performing human intelligence against his or her own organization.

Mastering Computer Security

So what are the basics of computer security? Many people will argue that there are countless technologies and disciplines within computer security, so there are countless basics. Again, though, basics should be independent of technologies.

With that in mind, there are two fundamental ways to break into (a.k.a hack) computers. They are simply: 1) take advantage of problems built into the software and hardware, and 2) take advantage in the way a user or administrator sets up and uses the computer or network.

Taking Advantage of Problems Built Into the Software

Concerning the way someone takes advantage of problems built into hardware or software, it is based on the fact that all software has bugs. Everyone can accept that there are bugs in software. Everyone has experienced a computer crashing or doing something annoying or unexpected. That is a software bug. Computer hardware also has software built into it, a.k.a firmware.

As all computer users experience, different bugs create different problems. Some bugs create elevated privileges or cause information leakage. These bugs are what are known as security vulnerabilities. According to the Computer Emergency Response Team (CERT), these security vulnerabilities are the cause of 30 percent of successful computer attacks.

In general, a computer has an operating system. An operating system is not a single computer program, but a set of thousands of computer programs that control the computer hardware as well as to interact with the application programs that give the computer a purpose. Every time you buy a printer or other piece of a computer, you have to add a "driver" which is essentially another computer program added to the operating system. A security vulnerability can exist in any of the programs comprising the operating system. The severity of the vulnerability depends on a variety of factors. It can cause minor damage, or possibly give an attacker full control of the entire system.

Then there are the application programs. They include word processors, spreadsheets, video games, Web browsers, and any other programs that you install on the computer to do more than to sit in a corner. While many readers might be thinking of this as only affecting PCs, even large computers such as mainframes have applications software.

While most people and organizations buy their applications software, most organizations also create their own software or have someone create it for them. For example, most Web sites are created with custom developed software. Also, while just about all companies will buy a database management system, they frequently write their own programs to access the data within the system.

Security vulnerabilities can exist in any software program. The resulting damage depends on the underlying bug. For example, a common bug for Web sites that provide database information is called a Structured Query Language (SQL) Injection Attack. SQL is a database language that is used to ask the database for information. If Web site software is poorly written, it can allow an attacker to enter his or her own SQL commands through the Web server and into the database, and retrieve more information than the Web site would otherwise allow.

An example of a security vulnerability that is built into an operating system is that versions of Windows 95 stored the user's password in a file on the computer. All you had to do was look in the file to steal the password.

Some software vulnerabilities are such that any attacker who can connect to the computer can completely take control. Other vulnerabilities require the victim to take an action, such as opening up a Microsoft Word file that contains an attack against a bug in Microsoft Word.

Again, all software has bugs and some of those bugs will be security vulnerabilities.

Does Microsoft Software Have More Vulnerabilities Than Other Software?

Fundamentally, the answer is maybe. However, this doesn't mean that a Microsoft system will be less secure than other software while in use. The underlying issue with the Microsoft Windows/Vista operating system is that it has a great deal of functionality built into it. It actually has much more functionality than a typical operating system. To have that functionality, there is more software. The more software, the more potential for bugs and, therefore, the more potential for security vulnerabilities.

This, however, doesn't mean that there has to be more security vulnerabilities. Even though people have tried, there has never been an operating system written with no security vulnerabilities. Microsoft has significantly improved their software practices over the last decade, and their operating systems have significantly lower rates of vulnerabilities than most other software.

Macintosh does have their commercials that make you believe that Macintosh computers are less susceptible to security vulnerabilities. The fact is that this may only be because fewer people use Macintosh computers and, therefore, they are significantly less attractive for hackers to target. Many vulnerabilities have been found in Macintosh computers and it has yet to be established that Macintosh's programming practices are more secure than Microsoft's.

Either way, the primary issue that determines how secure any computer is, is how well it is maintained. The Microsoft Update Service allows for free and automatic downloads of new security patches. If you enable the service, your computer is likely to be secure from most current attacks. If you compare a Macintosh computer that is not maintained well with a Windows computer that is well maintained and updated, the Macintosh computer will be much less secure. If the situation is reversed, the Windows computer would be less secure.

How Are These Bugs Found?

The issues with security vulnerabilities are that they are built into the software from the time that they are released. The assumption is that nobody knows that they are there in the first place. As with all software bugs, security vulnerabilities are found as people use and test the software. Sometimes people stumble on the vulnerabilities. After all, if you have hundreds of millions of people using something, someone will eventually do something that was not accounted for by the software.

Then there are people who look for software vulnerabilities. These are the hackers in the true sense of the word. The chapter that discusses the hacker community will have more details on this, but for now, we are talking about those people who use their custom testing tools or generic software test tools to find bugs in the software.

The nature of the "hacker" determines what happens with the vulnerability. If the hacker is a legitimate professional, they would report the problem to the software company and provide them with the information required to fix the problem. Then the software company has to actually fix the problem. Sometimes, while it might appear to be a simple fix, it might take weeks to fix the problem. A software vendor, like Microsoft for example, has to test their fix to make sure that it doesn't create a problem elsewhere in the software.

If the hacker has criminal intent, they would not disclose the information about the problem so that they can exploit it for their own purposes. Some people are ego driven, and they want to get the information out to gain the notoriety. In this case, people will be able to exploit the problem before it can be fixed.

Fixing Software Security Vulnerabilities

No matter what the software vulnerability, the software has to be rewritten and then replaced. It is basically that simple in concept. I say in concept, as many people and organizations do not update their software as it becomes available. Windows Update Service frequently looks for new software fixes to update. Other operating systems have similar features, however, it is all dependent on the users actually making use of the update system or otherwise looking for and installing the updates on their own.

Taking Advantage of How the Computer is Configured or Maintained

According to the CERT, the vast majority of attacks do not involve attacks that result from software bugs, but from otherwise secure software being set up, maintained, or used insecurely. For example, I lost track a decade ago as to how many passwords are the same as the user ID inside large companies. Default passwords on computer network devices also allow for compromise after compromise. Sometimes the passwords are easily guessable, like the story I told of a woman who had the user ID "kirk" and the password "captain."

Choosing bad passwords are not the only configuration errors. System hardening refers to setting computer options to make the computer secure. This first involves making sure that all of the appropriate software is updated, as previously described. Computer programs that are not needed are turned off. User groups are defined, and group members only get the minimal permissions that they need. Likewise, permissions are set for all files on the computer. In most cases, you also need to ensure that security software, such as anti-virus, anti-spam, and personal fire-walls, are loaded on the system. I am oversimplifying the process here, but there are very distinct things that need to be done to a computer to secure it.

Getting the computer secure in the first place is only a small step. From that point on, people use the computer system, and they can undo even the best security procedures. People can reset passwords or write their passwords next to a computer. Likewise, they can give the password away over the telephone, or respond to a phishing attack.

Administrators can also ruin security in a major way. There is a saying, "To err is human. To really screw things up takes an administrator." Administrators can create problems accidentally, naively, or purposefully changing computer settings that make the computer insecure. On some occasions, I have witnessed administrators make systems less secure because of frustration. For example, after installing a firewall and configuring it to be as restrictive as possible, the administrator started receiving complaints. As management started to add their support to the complaints, the administrators decided to just allow all network traffic in and out of the network. Of course, this made the firewall essentially useless, but they were able to say they had a firewall and didn't receive any more complaints.

How people construct a network can render security ineffective. For example, they can put critical computer systems outside of a secure network. People still place modems and backdoor connections onto networks, which basically bypasses some of the best security countermeasures. Unsecured wireless network routers allow people into your organization or home. Insecure laptops plugged into an otherwise secure network can bring in malicious software.

There are many ways to misconfigure a computer system or network. Just about all of these misconfigurations are well known, and therefore easy to exploit. Just as tools can be automated to look for bugs in software tools, most scanning tools also search for configuration vulnerabilities as well.

With the thousands of programs on a typical computer that are mostly written securely, there are an almost infinite number of ways to misconfigure that software. Using an automobile analogy: while they are composed of thousands of parts that can individually fail and cause an accident, all but a handful of crashes result from driver error of one form or another. That error can be that of other drivers. Similarly, on the Internet, you can do everything perfectly and be broadsided by the actions of others.

I must say that I believe that another type of configuration issue is not appropriately keeping software up to date. While it is true that the underlying problem is that there is a bug in the software, the fact is that the bug would be fixed and no longer a security threat if there was a process in place to proactively seek out and install software patches.

Studies by the Defense Information Systems Agency found that 97 percent of successful attacks against the Department of Defense were preventable. Outside of the Defense Department, the number is likely to be above 99 percent. This means that some reasonable human action would have prevented the attacks in all but a few rare occurrences.

Preventing the Configuration Vulnerabilities

Just like the system hardening addresses the software vulnerabilities, it should deal with the configuration issues. These documents are available for a variety of computer systems types at the NIST and NSA Web sites.

Can you Master Information Security?

Frankly, you don't really have to master information security to adequately protect yourself. If you can remember to address the basics, and not get overwhelmed by the technology underlying the basics, it is relatively easy to be secure enough that most attackers will move on to softer targets.

A layperson can secure themselves reasonably, but cannot, however, design a corporate security program or secure a large network. Becoming a master requires that you love what you are doing. It means that you want to understand what goes into the basics. It means that you study patterns in computer systems so that you can predict where vulnerabilities will be on new systems. Like a Martial Arts Master studies a variety of other martial arts to understand and improve their own art, an Information Security Master will study the business and technology so that they can improve their own skills.

Chapter 6

Knights
and Dragons

Many people who have seen my presentations know that I spend way too much time watching movies and television. I spend so much time watching movies and television that I looked for a way to make them tax deductible. I found a way when I started to see trends in shows and movies.

The one thing that I noticed was that in order to have a superhero, you needed a super villain. Without the super villain, there is no reason for the superhero. In each story about a brave knight, there had to be a dragon that was otherwise unstoppable. What type of story would it be if the only thing a knight has to do is kill weeds?

It would appear, though, that many people watch a lot of movies. To portray themselves as heroes, they create a dragon to go out to fight. Ronald Reagan was great at creating such imagery. He referred to the Soviet Union as the "Evil Empire." He created a dragon for the nation to focus on and rally behind. The radical Islamic world calls the United States the "Great Satan." Kim il Song uses the United States as a dragon to cement his image as the protector of North Korea.

George W. Bush has created imagery throughout his entire Presidency. His first dragon was the "Axis of Evil." Clearly Osama bin Laden was a clear dragon. When it became apparent that bin Laden was not going to be captured, Saddam Hussein became the dragon. When people criticized Bush's policies while the Republicans had control of Congress, they were the "Liberal Media." Then there was al Zarqawi, who was the leader of al Qaeda in Iraq. As I write this, Iran is being developed as the dragon.

I am not saying that these people weren't evil, but that they were used in a way to create imagery to solidify backing of policies or leaders. Frankly, the creation of the imagery was a brilliant political strategy.

Imagery is not necessarily limited to Republicans. President Clinton made the most inept use of imagery when he declared, "A teenager with a computer is more dangerous than a terrorist with a bomb." He said that in an effort to get support for his critical infrastructure protection strategies.

Osama bin Laden and al Qaeda have thrived off of the imagery. They love to be portrayed as an undefeatable enemy of the Great Satan. Every time people refer to bin Laden and al Qaeda as the greatest threat to the United States, it makes them seem even more powerful, and garners them even more support among radical Islam.

The FUD Factor

The reason that dragons work in the real world is that they create *fear*, *uncertainty*, and *doubt* (FUD). The more uncertain the populace is, the more they look for a knight to give them certainty. The more FUD there is, the more people will accept ridiculous security countermeasures. Frequently, security countermeasures can be completely useless, but they make people believe that something is being done.

Consider the reaction of the US government after the September 11 attacks. They went as far as banning tweezers on airplanes. The reason that the September 11 attacks were successful was because people were told to cooperate with hijackers and you will likely live through the experience. At the time, someone could just stand up and say that they had a bomb, and the whole plane would cooperate with them. It didn't matter whether the hijackers had a knife, gun, or tweezers. During September 11, people began to realize that you could no longer cooperate with hijackers. This is why the passengers of United Flight 93 rebelled against the hijackers. At this point, if anyone pulls out a pair of tweezers and tries to hijack a plane, you deserve to die if they are successful.

Whenever you hear people creating FUD, pay careful attention as they are trying to manipulate as many people as they can. There may be something reasonable to be concerned about, but you have to look at what they are trying to accomplish.

Dragons Forgive Incompetency

I remember a speech by Richard Clarke, then White House Counterterrorism chief. During the speech, he brought up the case of Operation Solar Sunrise. This was a case where the Deputy Secretary of Defense declared that the Department of Defense was experiencing "the most coordinated and sophisticated attack" that they had seen. Three weeks later, they arrested two teenagers from California.

A further investigation proved that these were two script kiddies in the truest sense of the word. All they did was download a tool that exploited widely known vulnerabilities off of the Internet, and made some basic modifications to it that allowed it to sequentially scan Department of Defense computers. When interviewed by various reporters, they were shown to be truly childish. Frankly, the US government should have been grossly embarrassed that these two teenagers were able to compromise any computer system under their care.

Instead, Clarke had to go around stating the Administration's storyline, "If two teenagers can do this, just imagine what a foreign adversary could do."

Instead of stating that the Department of Defense has done such a bad job protecting themselves that they mistook two clueless teenagers for sophisticated attackers, he makes the teenagers into little dragons to imply that there are even bigger dragons out there.

Basically, the Department of Defense shirked their responsibility for taking basic precautions, and created a dragon to blame the situation on. After all, even a powerful knight might sometimes lose to a powerful dragon. We have to forgive the knight, and support him, as he is our champion. If we don't have our champion, we have nobody, and having no champion is defeat.

What If You're Not a Knight?

If on the other hand you are not portraying yourself as a knight, if the dragon defeats you, it doesn't matter. Think about it. Nobody expects peasants to be able to protect themselves from a dragon. Most organizations that are compromised take the position that the hackers used advanced methods to compromise them. They portray themselves as peasants against a powerful dragon. Instead of admitting that they didn't protect themselves from widely known and preventable attacks, they portray the attackers as super-geniuses. They are basically trying to deflect responsibility for their lack of action.

The average person whose computer is successfully attacked, also frequently exhibits the same attitude. Even if the attack exploited widely preventable problems, people like to think of the hackers as geniuses. Even though the "victims" probably heard how to protect their computers time and time again, they still want to think of themselves as the victims of an evil genius.

Terrorists Really Aren't That Good

I will use terrorists as an example, since their imagery is so pervasive throughout the world. The fact of the matter is that hackers aren't that good either. Again, though, the media and politicians love to create a face of evil. There are plenty of examples of real dragons that go unseen.

In my book, *Spies Among Us*, I describe a case study where a group of former Special Forces operatives were able to blow up an airport within three days of being assigned the mission. When you read about terrorist operations, you find that they planned their attacks for over a year.

The 2006 case of the United Kingdom terrorist group that was planning to blow up several airplanes in flight using liquid-based explosives, is a quintessential example of this. It is still unknown as to when they began planning these attacks. The fact was that the terrorists were being watched for months, and even at the time of their arrest they were still apparently months away from the actual attack.

Special Forces operatives can execute similar attacks within a week. We are extremely lucky that terrorists are much less competent than they are made out to be.

With regard to hackers, the case is very similar. Most hackers do not have the incredible skills that they are portrayed as having. Again, I and the people I have been honored to work with have been able to take over major operations within hours, with very short planning cycles. Typical criminals and script kiddies take significantly longer to accomplish the same types of tasks. Unfortunately, though, most people and organizations leave themselves so vulnerable that even people with minimal skills can compromise them.

In the computer world, there are many real dragons out there. The most notorious includes the Chinese military, which is systematically scouring the Internet for any system that might contain anything valuable. They have been documented to be able to fully compromise a computer system and erase all of their tracks within 20 minutes. These people are extremely professional. This however doesn't mean that they are unstoppable.

The People You Really Have to Worry About

There really are very distinct classes of people to worry about with regard to "hackers," as they are generally known. They are broadly:

- Real computer geniuses
- Professionals
- Opportunists
- Script kiddies

Real Computer Geniuses

I already described that there are computer vulnerabilities built into software. However, it is not that the software developers knowingly release software with bugs. They are unknowingly written into the software. While some of the vulnerabilities become evident after widespread use, other vulnerabilities are discovered through detailed testing of the software by people who look specifically for security vulnerabilities. Frequently, these people have tools that should have been available to the developers. Sometimes the tools are custom developed. Either way, it takes a great deal of understanding of software.

These people can either be freelancers or do this work for hire. Freelancers seem to do it for the accolades that go with finding the vulnerabilities. The people who work for hire might work for a company that wants the accolades for the organization. Many security firms have become known only because of this type of work. Sometimes the organizations are criminal organizations, which hire people to find otherwise unknown vulnerabilities so that they can exploit systems at will. Other times, the organizations are government agencies that likewise want to exploit systems at will.

Professionals

In recent years, there has been a rise in the number of people who compromise computer systems for professional reasons. This group of people doesn't necessarily find new computer vulnerabilities, but they are expert at exploiting those vulnerabilities. Again, they are scientists in that they look at exploiting computer systems as a process. Many of the attacks are automated, where they just look for large volumes of computer systems and see if they are vulnerable to widely known attacks.

There is a growing rank of criminals that focus on computer crimes. These people have processes to compromise, or use compromised, systems for profit. Organized crime has also begun to follow the money into cyberspace, and have hired many people to commit crimes on their behalf. As also implied, foreign intelligence and military agencies around the world have created corps of people to focus on military and intelligence applications of compromising computers around the world. They are very good at what they do.

I should also include terrorist organizations in this category. They are beginning to realize that the Internet can be used to further their cause. While it is extremely unlikely that they will engage in cyberterrorism, they are beginning to use the Internet for recruitment, communications, and raising money. An arrest of an al Qaeda member in Indonesia also yielded an al Qaeda manual on computer crime. They realize that identity theft and crimes like Click Fraud can yield their organization millions of dollars for very little effort.

Opportunists

Opportunists are not professionals who devote their efforts to compromising computers. They are people who perform otherwise criminal actions that use computers as a tool of their crimes. Computers are so tied into everyday life that they are eventually tied to crimes. Remember that malicious insiders are the biggest malicious threat that organizations face. Since computers are so tied into everyday business functions, they are extremely likely to be used as a tool of a crime. Opportunists generally exploit computers as a layperson would. They use the access that they normally have. They might know or guess the password of a coworker, and exploit that. Sometimes, they might search the Internet to find out how to exploit a computer more thoroughly, or they might find people who can help exploit computers. Again, though, with opportunists, the computer is only an ad hoc tool to their endeavors.

Script Kiddies

I write a lot about script kiddies, so I should be clear about how I define them. As described, there are people who find computer vulnerabilities. Everyone else finds out about the vulnerability, and then someone writes a computer program to exploit the vulnerability. The program can be technically referred to as a "script." People who would be otherwise unable to compromise a computer without such scripts are known as script kiddies.

The term basically implies that the attacker has very little computer knowledge or skills. They compromise computers not because they're smart, but because their victims leave themselves vulnerable to even the most trivial attacks. Sadly, though, these people come across more than enough vulnerable systems. They can therefore cause a great deal of damage with little or no skill.

Look for Snakes, Not Dragons

Dragons are mythical beasts. Snakes are real and pervasive. They are among the most common poisonous animals in the world. Sometimes, though, people make snakes into dragons. Osama bin Laden is a snake, and a small snake at that. However, he is being made out to be a dragon. He is probably very appreciative of that.

While the voters apparently made terrorism the deciding factor in the 2004 presidential election, we saw tens of thousands of deaths from automobile accidents. Tens of thousands of people were killed during random crimes. Hundreds of thousands of people died from heart disease and other obesity-related causes. While I love donuts, donuts were clearly responsible for many more American deaths than terrorism.

All of this is proof that we are more worried about the mythical dragons than the common, everyday snakes. If you want to improve your security posture, you need to worry about the snakes.

Don't Suffer Death By 1,000 Cuts

All of the attention is given to dramatic attacks or other major events. The fact is that we lose so much on a daily basis to small things that we don't even consider. When looking at computers, consider how much time you waste having to go through and delete spam. Think about how many times your computer crashed, leaving you with data loss or at least the time to recover. Data losses occur regularly.

People likewise are terrified of some sort of wide-scale computer attack, yet natural disasters occur on a regular basis. Think about the damage that Hurricane Katrina caused to computer assets. There are many more hurricanes that caused billions of dollars of damage. Winter storms likewise cause major computer outages and widespread damage. We even have cases of a single tree falling down causing widespread power outages. Without power, computers cannot function.

So, if you want to really be concerned about security and risk, you have to look at the likelihood of events. Again, you have to focus your attention on the snakes, not the dragons.

Chapter 7

Cyberterrorism
is Not Effective

There has been a great deal of attention paid to the threat of cyberterrorists; so much so that I believe it is important to address this subject in a separate chapter. Again, when President Clinton made his statement that a teenager with a computer is more dangerous than a terrorist with a bomb, he was doing so to create attention for the threat of cyberterrorism.

The reality is that there is a potential problem with terrorists attempting to create damage through the use of computers. As I said in the previous chapter, terrorists have found some really good uses for the Internet: *recruitment*, *communications*, and *financing*. As it is so easy to create damage on the Internet, it is theoretically possible for terrorists to also create damage on the Internet.

However, the issue is that it is really easy to create damage on the Internet. More important is that few people have trust in computers to begin with.

When I took intelligence courses throughout my time with the NSA, one thing I learned was that there are specific definitions of warfare and related topics. For example, *warfare* is defined as the use of military force to achieve a political goal. It can then be extrapolated that *terrorism* is the use of fear, uncertainty, and doubt (FUD) to achieve a political goal.

For example, it can be stated that the terrorists who set off the Madrid subway bombings were successful in their terrorism goals. They were going for a political goal of getting Spain to withdraw from the multi-national force in Iraq. After the bombings, which occurred days before an election, the president was defeated and the successor withdrew Spanish troops from Iraq.

It is important to state that the goal of terrorism is to achieve terror, not damage. Frankly, these days it is really easy to create terror without creating damage. Put out a video threatening terrorism on a subway, and CNN and Fox News will jump all over it, and then everyone will be afraid to ride the subway.

On the other hand, just imagine if you threaten to take down computers. In the first place, few people have confidence in computers anyway. They are already used to computers crashing. Most importantly, it is not likely to affect the way they do business.

The reason is that to really create FUD, you need to threaten people's lives. In order to get people to change the way they behave, they have to think that their lives are in danger.

Anthrax vs. Nimda

I don't think that it was clearer to me how ineffective cyberterrorism could be than it was a week or two after the September 11 attacks. As many people might remember, this was the time that Anthrax laced envelopes were sent to a variety of locations around the country. The nation was terrified.

Think about how effective the attacks were. People were afraid to check and open their mail. That is an activity that is so fundamental to our daily lives.

Several days later, I received a call from a CNN reporter asking me to come into the studio and be interviewed about a new computer attack that was going on. The reporter said that the FBI is going to say that the computer attack is terrorist-related. I asked the reporter for details about the attack, and told him that it sounded nearly identical to the "Code Red" worm. He said that this one was called Nimda, and that since it was terrorist-related, CNN was going to cover it.

Two hours later, I received a call from the reporter that the interview was cancelled. He said that the FBI declared that Nimda was not terrorist-related, so it was not newsworthy to the higher ups at CNN. I replied that since Nimda was so similar to Code Red, Nimda would likely cause billions of dollars of damage just like Code Red. It was a major business story. The reporter stated that he knew this, but since it wasn't terrorist-related, random computer damage was not important enough.

While I don't want to minimize a single death, the fact is that Anthrax killed ten people over a two-month period of time. Again, many more people died from eating donuts during that same time period. Nimda went on to cost the world billions of dollars of damage, but it was only computer-related.

It is Easier to Blow Things Up

It is theoretically possible to create some potentially catastrophic damage through computer hacking. The issue is that the stars have to align for this to occur. There are very many things that are also well outside the control of the potential terrorist. So, even if a terrorist does find out a way to create some damage, it is not the easiest way to accomplish a terrorist act.

A terrorist might more easily be able to take down a piece of the infrastructure. While they might not be able to force a transformer to blow itself up, they may be able to take the generator down for a period of time. However, the damage is likely to be short term, as eventually the computers can be rebooted.

On the other hand, it is much easier to blow something up. There are many soft targets around the country. If you hack a transformer, it might be down for a few weeks. If you blow up a transformer, it will be out for six months. More importantly, the act of blowing something up creates a fear of death. Give people the impression that it can happen anywhere, and people around the country will be terrified.

What is a Terrorist?

Terrorists want to create FUD. Anytime you see someone creating FUD for any reason, anytime you hear someone telling you to be afraid, they are a terrorist.

Some healthy concern is fine, but all too often they are assisting the terrorists more than they are securing the country. You have to hear people put risk in perspective with the likelihood of attack. There is a terrorist threat, but extreme measures that are out of scope with the actual risk are creating the environment that the terrorists want.

Chapter 8

Common Sense
and Common
Knowledge

I once gave a presentation that the Wall Street Journal described as "hysterical." While I should be complimented by the comment, the fact was that it was a sign of a very sad state of affairs with regard to security.

The reason that my presentation was so funny was that it described "stupid users." Actually, there were a lot of stupid technical people described in my presentation as well, so we shouldn't just point fingers at the end users. I told the story of the password of "captain" on the account of "kirk." I told how I would walk into companies and employees would just hand me information. I described how I get security guards to open up locked doors for me, and how I get them to give me permanent access to the Computer Operations Center. I described how I sat down with an administrator, and the administrator started complaining about how everyone uses default passwords. He then went on to tell me what the passwords were. These are just a few of the situations that I run into.

The reason that the stories are so "hysterical" is that they defy common sense. After all, when you are sitting in an audience listening to a person who compromises security for a living, it is all put in context. Most people think that they would never be that stupid.

When I ask people if they would ever give a stranger their password, people clearly say, "No!" However, when I actually ask people for their password as a stranger, I inevitably get a password.

The fundamental issue is that of *common sense* vs. *common knowledge*. You cannot expect people to behave with common sense if they don't have a common knowledge.

If people do not have a grounding of common knowledge, they will not behave in a way that makes common sense. The reason why I say that it is a sad state of affairs that my stories are "hysterical," is that the security community has done a poor job of instilling common knowledge so that users can practice common sense.

I was recently on a conference panel on the subject of identity theft. The panel moderator asked how many people on the panel were taken in by a phishing attack. Nobody was. Likewise, when we talk to most people in the security community, very few people have been taken in by a phishing attack. There is clearly a common knowledge among security professionals. For some reason, though, there are more than enough people who don't have common knowledge or who don't exercise common sense.

There are many other areas where users don't demonstrate an understanding of common knowledge; Passwords, home users who don't properly secure their computers, keeping anti-virus software updated, and so on.

When there are widespread problems, there is clearly a failure in how the security community is delivering their message. In a corporate environment, good security awareness programs are required. When the general public is concerned, it is still unclear as to who is ultimately responsible for security awareness.

Wanting Benefit Without the Associated Costs

It is my opinion that the current state of poor computer and information security is that nobody wants to be responsible. This includes companies, individuals, and government. For example, the computer owner is ultimately responsible for how their computer is configured. However, if they configure or maintain their computer insecurely, they generally don't believe that they should be responsible for the resulting losses. Likewise, if an attacker uses their computer to attack a third party, they don't want to be liable for those actions.

With regard to companies, despite the fact that Internet Service Providers (ISPs) make a profit for selling Internet service, they don't want to accept responsibility for providing a safe Internet experience, like the simple filtering out of clear attack traffic. Companies that accept credit cards over the Internet fight government regulation for requirements of securing the credit card information. They don't want to be held liable for their own potential poor security, but they do want all the profits that come with taking credit cards over the Internet.

There are many factions of the US Government that truly want to help the situation. However, they don't want to accept or assign responsibility. For example, while the Federal Trade Commission (FTC) has made some highly visible prosecutions, the prosecutions have been few and only when the case is extremely public and egregious. They are not taking any proactive steps to require companies to behave securely. While the FTC is also putting a great deal of information up on the Internet with regard to how to prevent identity theft, the reality is that the information just sits there. Likewise, Congress is not willing to assign definitive responsibility to anyone with regard to protecting any elements of the Internet or consumers.

Compare the situation to cars. Users are required to properly maintain their automobiles, or they can be fined and the cars impounded. Companies are required to keep all of their vehicles safe, or they can be fined and the vehicles impounded. Government agencies are required to keep the roads in good repair. Likewise, their own vehicles must be properly maintained.

There is clear assignment of responsibility at all levels. While it can be argued that public safety is involved with automobiles, the fact is that tens of billions, if not hundreds of billions, of dollars are lost each year due to easily preventable computer crimes.

Without responsibility, people have little incentive to learn common knowledge. I am actually going to contradict what I said before by now saying that I think that most people have actually been exposed to common knowledge. The big problem is that many people choose to ignore the information as they are exposed to it. Some people close their ears immediately when they hear a computer is involved, thinking that they will never understand the information. More people just don't care because they think they will never be a victim. Given that there is little responsibility imposed on people and organizations, maybe it could be argued that they don't have to care.

The reality is that you are not going to change the world by yourself. What you can do is assign responsibility where you can. For example, if you are in a company, you can *enforce* corporate policies. Many companies have information security policies that are either not enforced or toothless. It is not unreasonable to say that after a second violation of security policies, people will be fired. While security at NSA, where I began my career, was not perfect, the fact that people could lose their jobs and possibly go to jail did make NSA exponentially more security aware in practice than just about all other organizations in the world. I can tell you there is no special security gene in people who work at NSA. It is just that since the penalties are so clear, people pay attention when they hear about security regulations, and do their best to practice the appropriate behaviors.

If you have children and you find them giving out improper information over the Internet, they should be punished severely and privileges taken away. After all, it could mean their life.

When people have a sense of responsibility, they will behave securely. Unfortunately, most people do not have any responsibility, which is the underlying cause of security problems.

Some People Are Just Stupid

As I wrote earlier, I watch a lot of television. One of my favorite shows is *Judge Judy*. In a recent episode, one woman was suing another because the defendant in the case advertised for a room-mate on craigslist.com. A person from Nigeria replied to the ad and said that they wanted the room, but they need money orders cashed so they can afford to move the United States. The money orders were sent to the defendant, who asked her friend, the plaintiff, to cash the money orders. The money orders were cashed. The defendant then wired the money to Nigeria. Several weeks later, the bank took the money out of the plaintiff's account saying that the money orders were forged.

What was even worse was that during the case, the defendant said that she does intend to pay off her friend, because she recently received an e-mail telling her that a long lost relative died and that she is to receive a multimillion-dollar inheritance. She told Judge Judy that she is paying the legal fees and taxes, so the money can be released. There was an audible gasp from the audience. You can guess how Judge Judy decided.

For some reason, many people are afraid to acknowledge that some people are just stupid. I recently went through Scuba Instructor training, and the teacher's favorite phrase was, "You can't stop stupid." He was referring to the fact that no matter how many times you tell people that their behavior can jeopardize their lives, some people will specifically do the things you tell them not to do. Then, when those people are injured through their own stupidity, they will try to sue anyone they can. Therefore, there was a lot of instruction as to how to document training.

Just as a certain percentage of the general population will be criminals (as is discussed in the next chapter), a certain percent of the population is just stupid. You need to acknowledge this and put this into your plans. Likewise, I strongly advise that you clearly set expectations and punishment for people under your responsibility. Then you must enforce the expectations and punishment. Stupidity must be figured into your plans. It is critical to understand that stupid people don't like to acknowledge that they are stupid, and therefore look for as many people as possible to blame.

Stupid is not limited to end users. The fact is that there are many administrators and other computer personnel who aren't the brightest people in the world. You can give them as much training as possible, yet they will consistently do things that damage operations. More importantly, given the access that administrators have, they can quickly compromise the security of the entire organization.

I am not stating that anyone who falls victim to some type of attack or makes a few mistakes is stupid. All people have bad moments, no matter how smart they are. Again, though, it is critical to acknowledge that some people will frequently do the wrong thing, even if there is otherwise common knowledge and common sense to the contrary. Despite the fact that this may be politically incorrect, it must be acknowledged.

The Wizard of Oz

One of my most popular presentations is "What the Wizard of Oz Says About Information Security." To make a long story short, while most people think the moral of the movie, *The Wizard of Oz*, is "There's no place like home," the real moral is you have what you're looking for. You just don't know it or know how to use it.

I think this statement is true in many disciplines, and especially security. As I previously stated, more than 97 percent of security incidents are completely preventable. The reason they are not prevented is because people did not make use of the countermeasures that they had access to. There are many countermeasures that people don't activate or otherwise make use of. For example, Windows Update Service can render many attacks moot proactively, if configured to run automatically. From an administration perspective, all common operating systems have the ability to require users to create strong passwords. Internet Explorer 7 can warn people when websites are being spoofed. McAfee Site Adviser performs similar functions.

Despite the fact that I am a big advocate for security awareness programs, few of them have been shown to be effective. For example, I spoke with a person who previously worked in eBay's Information Technology (IT) security department. He bemoaned how eBay spent millions of dollars on security awareness programs, yet eBay did not see any significant decrease in their members falling victim to fraud. Again, it was not through lack of trying.

I think that no matter how good awareness programs are, there are just too many stupid people out there to rely on them. For example, even if 99.9 percent of eBay users do the right thing, that still leaves upwards of 250,000 people who will fall victim to some type of fraud, costing millions of dollars in damage.

For that reason, I believe that we have to start using the security that is ubiquitous to our computers. Extending the automobile analogy I started, people know to put on their seatbelts and lock their doors when they get in their car. They know to look around as they leave their parking spot. They pay attention to traffic lights and road signs. They stay away from bad neighborhoods. They stay within the lines on the road and watch for other drivers. Aren't there an infinite number of ways that people can kill themselves or others in a car?

People don't care about how complicated the mechanics are of the car. This doesn't even enter their thought processes. Safety features of the car are ubiquitous. More importantly, they accept the role of common sense and regular maintenance. They don't challenge the fact that they have to put gasoline in their car. They accept that they need emissions inspections on a regular basis, as well as the fact that they have perform preventative maintenance, like changing the oil and other fluids in the car. These are the costs of owning a car.

Unfortunately, people and organizations don't want to accept that, just like cars, computers need to have regular maintenance. Computers are as critical to most people's lives as their cars, if not more so. Computers need to have their operating systems and other software updated on a regular basis. People need to spend money on updating the anti-virus software licenses just like they change their oil. The good part about all of this is that these functions are now generally automated. They only require the user to enable them.

There is so much out there to help people protect themselves. All they need to do is find out about them.

Chapter 9

Never Underestimate the Stupidity of a Criminal

While the previous chapter highlighted the stupidity of many users, the good news is that many criminals are even more stupid. For example, a few teenagers broke into my garage and stole my wife's wallet from a car. I decided to do some basic investigating and called all credit card companies to find out where her cards might have been used by the crooks. I quickly learned that they charged gas at a gas station in my city. That was the most specific information that they had.

I thought that I might have been dealing with some experienced criminals, as they tend to take credit cards to gas stations that take credit cards at the pump, to test out the card without having to interact with a person.

I decided to find the specific gas station, as the station might have had video cameras, and to go through the trash at the station, since smart thieves toss stolen goods they don't need in the trash at the first opportunity to get rid of evidence.

There are nine gas stations in the city, and as luck would have it, it was the last one I went to. I had the station attendants show me their credit card records at the time I was told the transaction was made and found the credit card number. I asked the current attendant on duty if they had a video of the night, and they didn't. I then asked who was there at the time of the transaction. They told me it was a woman that was there overnight, and said they would call her.

I did receive a call an hour later from the attendant on duty at the time of the transaction, and it turned out that not only did she remember the transaction, she knew exactly who the thief was. It turns out that it was three people. Two of them previously worked at the gas station, and one was fired because he was suspected of stealing things from cars in their shop. While using the "Pay at the Pump" feature, he actually went to talk to the attendant, because he thought she might see a name associated with the credit card used come up on her screen and see it wasn't his credit card. He told her that he was using his grandmother's card.

Basically, I wrapped up the criminals with a bow for the police, who was actually investigating two of these people for a variety of other thefts in the area. There was nothing especially brilliant that I did in this case. The thieves were just incredibly stupid in what they did after the theft. If the police would have put in the same minimal level of effort on the investigation of one of the other crimes these people were suspected of, they would have likely caught them before they got to my garage.

While the above case is clearly the case of imbeciles, I have seen similar levels of stupidity in many cases of major crimes. For example, in one case I investigated a break-in to a banking computer system that processes funds transfers; actually a lot of fund transfers.

I started to investigate in detail what the attacker was doing. I found many back doors in the system. Most importantly, there was some major software being loaded onto the system. After examining everything, it turned out that the person was actually a script kiddie who didn't even know what he broke into. He was putting up a warez site on the system.

A warez site is the term for an Internet site that contains pirated software and frequently hacking tools. The person created a system that allows people post and download software. They even put a note on the system to the effect: "This is my system. Please don't try to hack it as you are only compromising the good I am trying to do for all. Don't ruin it for other people."

It was almost comical. This person broke into a computer system that processed billions of dollars a year, and they didn't even realize it. They committed a major felony for the purpose of satisfying their ego by helping criminal's pirate software and otherwise break into other computers. They could have went to jail for a long period of time.

During other bank robbery investigations, I saw that the sophisticated criminals also rely on the stupidity of other criminals. In one investigation, I was tracking the activities of a person that we assumed, and found that to be a correct assumption, to be affiliated with the Russian Mafia. He was a very advanced "hacker" who knew many sophisticated techniques. He also used the bank infrastructure against them.

I watched this person who went in through one of the bank's electronic connections, and went out through others to cover his tracks. One of the things that was interesting to watch was when this criminal would go to hacker bulletin boards and other online gathering places. Frequently, this person pretended to be a teenage girl. Of course, all of the other hackers were all over him, or her as they thought. The criminal would chat all of the other hackers up to try to see how advanced they were. He would chide them to see what sort of access they might have illicitly obtained. Script kiddies love to brag, and even better, this criminal provided them with a girl to brag to, who seemed to understand what they were talking about and even acted impressed.

I was truly impressed with this criminal, as he masterly manipulated all of the script kiddies into divulging new attack strategies, systems that he could use as jumping points for other crimes, compromised accounts on banks around the world, and other access points to many banks, including my target. Clearly my watching his activities was very educational for me. More important, it allowed me to collect a wide variety of intelligence on vulnerable targets, that included my client as well as dozens of other companies around the world.

This criminal also used a variety of other ruses to get script kiddies to divulge information. Again, he took advantage of the stupidity of other criminals. In some cases, he would find people who claimed to be "elite" and then call them stupid. To try to prove they are "elite," these script kiddies would brag about their conquests. When the criminal says, "Well if you are elite, you would have access to Bank X," the script kiddie would sometimes say, "I have Admin there." The criminal would challenge the script kiddie to prove it, and the kiddie would give them the specific address of the computer system as well as the user ID and password for the account.

The criminal in this case could have just as easily have been a police officer on a sting.

Dateline's To Catch a Predator series, which gets Internet child predators to come to a sting operation, is another example of how criminals can be stupid. At least one of the people caught by the sting showed up to a later sting. They never learn.

Time and time again, I investigate crimes that are almost comical. As I previously wrote, most crimes should have been easily prevented. This means that criminals don't need to be very intelligent to commit their crimes.

However during the investigation of crimes, I have to assume the worst. I have to assume that the perpetrator might be part of an organized crime ring, foreign intelligence agency, or maybe even part of the Chinese Titan Rain team. Ironically, there are many times that these perpetrators might even appear to be script kiddies. The reason is that the smart criminals might not want to stand out. Savvy administrators and security personnel regularly encounter so many "stupid" criminals, that they tend to just ignore the attacks because they assume that they can just stop the amateur criminals in their tracks and move on to supposedly more important things.

The savvy criminals move on to other tactics and raise the sophistication of attacks. It is only after you observe what a hacker does after they get into the system that you can make a true determination of their intent and level of expertise. Admittedly, truly professional attacks are few and far between, and there are many more stupid criminals than good ones.

As I also mentioned, a lot of crimes involve insiders abusing their privileges. While these people know their organization to a certain extent, the reality is that they are not aware of, or consider, all countermeasures that their organization may have. Given this, many insiders leave so many blatant tracks, that if you get over the betrayal factor, the crimes seem comical.

One time I was asked to advise a company where the information security manager was implicated in posting unflattering corporate information to the Internet. The corporate staff believed that it was the systems administration staff trying to discredit the security staff due to ongoing investigations of the Chief Information Officer (CIO) and administration staff.

It turns out that while the administration staff was savvy enough to forge computer addresses and a variety of other data that generally implicated the information security manager, the administrators failed to consider that the access control systems recorded every time a person entered and exited the building. Additionally, surveillance cameras videotaped all entrances. Given the internal power struggles, though, they went to an additional level of pulling cell phone company records, which are able to track the location of an individual's cell phone, and essentially the person.

Therefore, the administrators were eventually charged with a variety of crimes that went well beyond the original issues. Even though the administrators were relatively smart, their actions were naïve with regard to the wealth of information that is available about people's movements.

Frequently, the criminals want to put intrigue into the mix. They watch more movies than I do to look for ideas on how to commit their crimes. They don't realize that most movie spies and criminals are as realistic as the tooth fairy. For example, in a case where a Coca Cola employee and two accomplices intended to sell Coca Cola secrets to a competitor, they did everything like they were part of a spy novel.

First, they chose to try to sell a new secret formula to Pepsi. That is too obvious, on top of the fact that as a large American company they are more likely to turn in such an amateur attempt of industrial espionage, rather than to be part of it. Then the criminals wanted to have secret meetings in locations out of spy novels. When it came time to receive payment, they wanted the money as unmarked bills in a shoebox. While I am not going to provide suggestions as to how they could have been better criminals, they were clearly watching too many movies.

These are just some sample cases of stupid criminals. While you have to assume that the criminals are potentially highly skilled with unlimited resources, you shouldn't be surprised when it seems like it is too easy to catch the criminals, because they are frequently stupid. Again, while I would like to make myself out as some expert for identifying the criminals who broke into my garage within an hour, I used extremely basic investigative techniques. Ninety percent of me catching the criminals was due to the fact that they were just stupid.

When you are in the process of investigating crimes against yourself or your organization, I should first state that you need to make sure that you don't ruin the investigation, either by destroying evidence or doing something that is potentially going to overshadow the crime itself. For example, in the Hewlett-Packard (HP) scandal where HP executives were accused of a variety of crimes in an attempt to try to find out the source of a boardroom leak, there was a potentially serious crime committed; that being the leak of boardroom information. However, in trying to investigate the crime, HP used methods that overshadowed the crime itself.

Untrained investigators can also destroy or contaminate evidence that might be used in the future in a criminal prosecution. For example, if there is a potential computer-related crime, the first thing you need to do is a complete backup of the system. This way criminals cannot say that you tampered wit the evidence to frame them. Likewise, you could potentially overwrite critical evidence in the computer's memory. For example, deleted files might appear to be unavailable, but it is actually trivial to recover the data, assuming it is not overwritten.

There is a Difference Between Being Good and Being Effective

Despite the fact that many criminals you face are either stupid or otherwise not very talented, they can be very effective. The sad fact is that there are so many poorly secured computer systems and so many people who demonstrate poor security awareness, that it is easy to find a target. Persistence and the information available on the Internet is more than enough for a would be criminal to overcome a lack of skill or talent.

The general public is essentially creating a dragon out of a gnat when they are awed by most computer crimes. A teenager who picks up a knife and stabs someone is not a master criminal. They can effectively kill someone, but it doesn't imply they have the medical knowledge of a Hannibal Lechter. It is the same situation for computer criminals. Finding a tool on the Internet and letting the tool run on a computer doesn't make that person a computer genius.

Understanding your Adversary

My friend Stan, the GRU defector, told me how from the age of 11, while he was attending a Soviet military school, a great deal of training was focused on understanding the American mindset. Throughout his education, he was told that a war with the United States was inevitable, and that as a future soldier, he must understand how Americans think. He was exposed to as much American culture as possible. There was, of course, a great deal of propaganda embedded in all of the teachings, but he knew much more about America by the time he graduated high school than most American high school graduates.

When Stan moved on as a GRU operative to target China, he likewise learned a great deal about Chinese history and culture. He was extremely successful as a GRU operative in both the United States and China, because he understood the importance of understanding his adversaries.

Stan is actually very specific in his use of the word "adversary" and not "enemy." From a geopolitical perspective, everyone is essentially an adversary. For example, while China and the United States would generally be considered enemies of Russia, they might periodically cooperate with Russia, if only to get together against each other. Even if the countries are on the same side at points in time, they will always be adversarial.

The term, enemy, also has a large amount of emotional baggage attached to it. People tend to hate their enemies. Adversary is a less emotional term. You do not want to get emotional in the course of doing your job. It clouds your judgment and might make you behave irrationally.

For example, it is easy to hate someone who steals your identity. However, the hate will make you focus on retribution, not the problems at hand. If you can determine how the identity thief is behaving, you can take more proactive steps in limiting the damage they intend to cause.

When my wife's purse was stolen, I focused on categorizing the thieves and how they might behave, instead of dwelling on them as enemies. That is what allowed me to retrace their steps and determine their identities.

There are many types of adversaries that we might face in the information world, and it is important to understand how they might behave. What follows are some broad categories of adversaries in no particular order. I do not intend to be completely thorough, as that would be too deep for the context of this book. Again, *Spies Among Us* has a more thorough discussion of adversaries.

Insiders

Insiders are your biggest adversary, no matter what environment you are in. I am assuming that you are well aware of countless cases of insiders going bad. Sometimes they do it because they are upset with their employer. Sometimes they get desperate and need money and take what they have access to. Sometimes they just want excitement. Whatever the reason, there are people who will do malicious acts.

Scott Charney, currently a Chief Strategist at Microsoft and previously chief of the Department of Justice's Computer Crime and Intellectual Property Unit, came up with what he calls his Charney Theory. Basically it is, "At any point in time, 3 percent of the population will do wrong if given the opportunity."

While I would like to think that the percentage is high, it acknowledges the fact that there are some people who will abuse the trust that they are given.

Probably the biggest threat that insiders pose is not malicious in nature. Everyone makes mistakes, and those mistakes have a cumulative effect of a major loss. I can personally attest to the fact that I accidentally deleted files that set back projects. Some people accidentally lean on the power switch. When administrators and other systems personnel make mistakes, their accidents can be devastating. Small programming errors have taken down portions of the telecommunications infrastructure. Otherwise inconsequential acts can cost millions of dollars.

MICE

As I mentioned before, espionage and human intelligence is a science, not an art. Human Intelligence operatives have been trained to identify people whom they can manipulate. Once they find a potential "agent," they then go through a process of desensitizing a person to their actions.

The acronym used by intelligence operatives for their marks is MICE, which stands for *money, ideology, coercion,* and *ego*. Money is fairly obvious. Someone who wants money and is morally ambiguous, is a highly potential mark. Ideology means that a person is morally opposed to their organization, or is morally sympathetic to yours. Coercion is essentially blackmail. Find something that you can hold against a person, and they can be very easy to manipulate. You just have to keep testing them to see how far you can push them.

Ego is extremely effective. The person thinks that they are smarter than everyone else. They tend to think that they are better than everyone else. A trained operative only has to stroke the person's ego, and they can get them to do just about anything.

Also associated with this is the process of desensitizing a person to their actions. When information is computer based, it is especially easy. A trained operative will get a person to divulge benign information at first, and then slowly elevate the stakes. Along the way, they will also change the person's language patterns. They are not stealing something, they are copying it. The information isn't important anyway. A lot of people have access to the information. Besides that, the company isn't paying you enough to protect the information anyway. A person who is also getting money finds it easier and easier to rationalize their actions.

As we discuss other threats, what you will find is that language patterns are the best indicators of a criminal. They will blame others. They will down play their own actions. They will use words for their actions that make criminal actions trivial. We will discuss this further when we talk about the criminal mindset.

Competitors

Everyone has competitors of one form or another. It can be one company against another. A coworker can be considered a competitor. Depending on the nature of the competitor, they can present varying levels of risk to you. Some competitors have significantly more resources than others. If you have foreign competitors, they may have the support of their government's national intelligence agencies.

Competitors can want a variety of information. They might want to steal your trade secrets. They might want to steal your customer list. They could want to know the status of your ongoing projects. They could just ask questions of people to get the information they want. They might hire private investigators. They could resort to illegal actions. They might try to be clever, and put together job interviews. The tactics they use can be benign, egregious, and/or criminal.

When you are dealing with foreign competitors, you must realize that the definition of what is legal and ethical in the United States may be completely different elsewhere. You cannot rely on your own impression as to what is right an wrong and expect others to behave the same way.

Foreign Intelligence Agencies

At a recent meeting of bank security managers, there was resounding agreement that foreign intelligence agencies were a major threat to their banks. In their case, banks provide a lot of information that can be used to monitor criminals, terrorists, and so on. Banking records can also help uncover the identity of undercover operatives, if you know what to look for.

Most countries acknowledge that what's good for its businesses is good for the financial wellbeing of the country as a whole. For that reason, they might target international companies to steal information to give to their domestic companies. Sometimes they are looking for specific technologies, such as defense-related technologies. Foreign intelligence agencies can put essentially unlimited resources against a person or an organization. Some intelligence agencies get their operatives to get jobs inside companies. More frequently, they will recruit an insider who already has access to the information that they are looking for.

Organized Criminals

Organized crime has recently realized that there is a lot of money in cyberspace. Being purely profit driven, they have followed the money. Their initial forays into cyberspace involved getting payoff money from "cybercriminals." Mafia gangs in the former Soviet Republics would find people making money and demand their cut, which is their traditional way of doing business. The more savvy mafia groups started their own cybercriminal efforts by hiring former intelligence personnel or out-of-work computer professionals. Sometimes, they actually watch the hacker community and identify people with real talent. They use these people to run a wide variety of online extortion attempts as well as other criminal endeavors, such as outright stealing of money.

Organized crime came up with some of the more effective methods of stealing money. For example, they would steal credit card numbers and then charge the cards very small amounts, like $9.95 per month. While that might not seem like a lot of money, with hundreds of thousands of compromised credit cards these small amounts quickly add up to millions of dollars. More importantly, relatively few victims notice the scam. Even if they do, the money is so small that the banks won't bother investigating.

Mafia gangs and drug cartels are quickly realizing that there is more to do than to just steal money. They are using the Internet and other resources to improve their operations. Of course, though, these people have unlimited resources and use those resources for their own financial benefit. Any crime to that end is fair game.

Criminals

As previously discussed, since computers are integral to business as a whole, many crimes might target or use computers, whether or not the intent is to compromise computers. Just as cars are used as tools in crimes, so to can a computer be used in a crime. Criminals who use a computer as a casual part of their crime, don't have to be computer geniuses, as people who poorly maintain their computers make it easy for anyone with minimal research to successfully do whatever criminal act they choose to.

For these people, the computer is a casual tool to commit their crime. The good part about this is that they likely will do very little to cover their tracks. This makes it easy to potentially catch these people, if anyone is looking.

Cybercriminals

Cybercriminals have truly evolved in recent years. These are criminals whose crimes purely involve making money via computers.

They have generally been around since the Internet began. These are hackers who early on realized that they spent so much time on their computers that they could make money from it. The crumbling of the Soviet Union led to a rise of a new breed of computer criminal. These people then went on to perform a wide variety of fraud, extortion, and other crimes. Given the laws in these areas, these people were not necessarily criminals in their own countries. There is no risk to them, unless of course organized crime wants a share of their income.

Then there are the script kiddies who have grown up. Much like the early cybercriminals, financially motivated computer crimes are a natural progression for them. They don't necessarily have to be very good at what they do. Again, we make it very easy for them.

More recently we have seen an entire criminal infrastructure develop. Some cybercriminals focus on creating botnets. Other people rent those botnets to send out spam. Some people use the botnets for phishing to steal credit card numbers. They can then sell those credit card numbers through other criminal services that broker them.

Script Kiddies

I have mentioned script kiddies many times, and I won't dwell on them too much here. Script kiddies are motivated by their own ego. They want to feel special, and taking over a computer gives them the significance that they are looking for. They are very immature in what they are doing.

The damage they cause varies. Frequently, their crimes include defacement of Web sites. Sometimes they get into computer systems, and they can't think of anything better to do than just delete files and otherwise create damage. The critical enablers for their crimes include an Internet connection and too much time on their hands.

While these people are amateurs and should generally be considered low risk threats, they can create a great deal of damage. More importantly, they help shield the actions of other criminals.

The Criminal Mindset

I previously mentioned MICE and how intelligence operatives identify potential dupes as well as how they get these dupes to rationalize their behaviors. Criminals think differently than the average person. While they can sometimes hide their intent, their language patterns can give them away.

For example, police interrogators are trained to pick up when a suspect dehumanizes their victims. They refer to the victim with pronouns instead of their proper nouns. For example, a child abuser refers to their victim as "the child" vice naming them.

Criminals also rationalize or downplay their actions. When I interviewed William Gaede, who was infamous for stealing the early Pentium chip designs worth billions of dollars, for my book, *Corporate Espionage*, he claimed that he never committed a crime. His general contention was that since he never stole a physical document and never denied Intel access to their information, he never "stole" anything. During a debate with infamous hacker, Kevin Mitnick, I was essentially asked why I didn't believe he was "reformed" as he claims. I pointed out that he refers to phone phreaking, the term for hacking the phone system, as a "hobby." Phone phreaking is a felony, not a hobby.

Generally, criminals believe that they are smarter than the rest of the population. They frequently believe that as a superior person, they are entitled to what they steal. It is their belief that it is the fault of the victims for leaving themselves so vulnerable. Essentially, they perceive themselves as predators in a world of prey.

When they are caught, criminals downplay their crimes. Given that they think they are so intelligent, they blame their capture on the betrayal or actions of others. They blame victims for turning them in. They believe that the police are wasting their time on their actions, because there are so many other real criminals out there.

The difference between stupid criminals and smart criminals is that the smart criminals have a stronger sense of reality. Smart criminals know their actions are criminal. They go through tremendous lengths not to get caught. They are not arrogant, and they respect law enforcement and their victims. They know that simple mistakes can get them caught. I previously quoted Scott Charney and his Charney Theory that a certain percentage of people will commit a crime if given the opportunity. He has another quote that is relevant: "Only the bad ones get caught."

Hiring Hackers

When I previously mentioned the Colverdale teenagers, who were declared to be the source of the most coordinated and sophisticated attacks the Department of Defense (DoD) has ever seen, I mentioned how they really demonstrated very little skill. Yet, people were commenting on the case that the right punishment for these people is to make them fix all the damage that they caused. From a technical perspective, the thought is absurd, and sadly even many computer professionals don't understand why.

Let me use an analogy. Let's say a teenager picks up a knife and stabs someone right through the heart. Do you think that the appropriate punishment includes making that person perform surgery to fix the damage that they did? It is clearly absurd.

Fundamentally, the reason is that heart surgery is a very difficult skill to master. It is much easier to damage something than it is to fix it. The skill set is tremendously different.

Similar analogies include, should a person who drives a car into a wall be tasked with fixing the car? Can a person who takes a baseball bat and smashes a window fix the window? Why then is there an assumption that a person who knows how to damage a computer can also fix a computer?

A computer is a very complicated device with hundreds of thousands of files. Again, it is infinitely more difficult to secure a computer against all possible attacks, than to find a single attack against a vulnerable system.

Hackers demonstrate no relevant skills to security work. Some people may argue that they can at least perform penetration testing. That again is a completely absurd thought. In the first place, penetration testing potentially gives the tester access to an entire organization. This includes every bit of sensitive information in the company. How can anyone give someone who basically is acknowledging to have performed criminal acts in the recent past, access to the information?

Also, as I already mentioned, the best penetration testers have been long-term system administrators who battled hackers. They know the ins and outs of computer systems, and they have shown themselves to be trustworthy.

Another issue is that things can potentially go very wrong. While administrators have had to deal with problems their whole career, hackers don't care about the problems that they cause in the process. The career administrators know that they have to protect the systems as they break into them. For example, Mark Abene, a.k.a Phiber Optik, one of the more infamous hackers of the 1990s with multiple arrests and convictions, got work as a security consultant. I must admit, though, that he was much more talented than a typical script kiddie. During one of his "consulting" jobs, he ran a hacking program that went wrong. It basically started downloading password files from all over the Internet, greatly embarrassing the client and all others involved. Instead of taking responsibility for his actions, he claimed that it was the fault of people who didn't properly secure their computers, not his. No, it is the fault of a hacker not assuming the obvious, that computers might be insecure. Remember what I said about the criminal mindset.

It is possible that an unskilled security consultant might have made the same mistakes, however, the incident would not have been as embarrassing for all concerned. Either way, even if you somehow rationalize a criminal's actions for them, you still cannot justify the questionable skills. To summarize it best, you must hire resumes, not rap sheets.

Your Kids are Not as Smart as You Think

A critical issue that needs to be addressed, much more than hackers, is children. The most dangerous misconception I hear is that children are computer savvy. Many adults seem to believe that children are very aware of computer issues. This is a very dangerous belief to have about your children.

It is very true that children are more comfortable with computers. However, it doesn't mean that they are more security aware. Their only two concerns are potentially to make sure their parents don't know what they're up to, and creating and protecting their image.

Lance Hayden, a former CIA operative and PhD candidate at the University of Texas, performed a study about what college students consider privacy. The results had little to do with what most people would consider privacy. Teenagers and students through their early twenties thought of privacy as protecting information that makes them look bad. These people were more than happy to post information about where they live, their hobbies, hangouts, schedules, and so on. When Hayden had students research themselves from an intelligence/stalking perspective, very quickly the students were horrified and immediately wanted to find out how to get the information off the Internet. Again, these people were supposedly computer savvy.

Young people are computer savvy, but again, not security aware. It baffles me that people to this day still claim to be intimidated by computers. They have been using computers for a much longer period of time than their children, yet they want to be purposefully ignorant. This endangers their children.

Parents need to learn about MySpace, FaceBook, and the like. They must learn about Instant Messaging and the like. I am very angered by people suing MySpace, because their children were attacked, because of information that the children put on the Internet. I call this the "Bad Parents' Lawsuit." These parents basically are arguing that computer services should keep better tracks of their children than they are.

Children are children. They use the Internet like they use toys. They learn to do with it what they want. Again, they know how to use computers, not secure them. Children want to look cool. Thinking children know more than that, makes you the foolish one.

Chapter 10

Information Security
Is INFORMATION
Security

Throughout the book I imply that information security implies much more than computer security. As I said before, computers are essentially worthless.

In a recent local news story, a young couple had their house robbed. The reporter went on to talk about the loss of jewelry, silverware, televisions, and so on. However, when the reporter asked the couple about the loss, the only thing they really wanted back was their laptop computers. As the interview went on, it became apparent the woman really didn't care about her outdated computer, but her doctoral dissertation and associated data that was on the computer that she was working on for years.

Again, the hardware and software on a computer is a depreciating asset. The woman clearly could have bought a better computer for a cheaper price. However the effort associated with writing her dissertation was priceless. I would dare to say that this is true for everyone.

If someone steals your computer, would you think, "Damn, now I have to buy a new computer," or "What about all the pictures and bank information that I have on the computer?" For this reason, it is important to protect information in all of its forms.

The chapter defining risk highlighted the different areas of vulnerabilities. Those vulnerabilities apply to all forms of information. Information can be computer-based, hardcopy, verbal, or otherwise physical.

Clearly, verbal information can take many forms. It could be conversations. Any time someone speaks, someone else can be listening. It can also be telephone conversations. Telephone conversations can be intercepted in a variety of ways, as has become well known with the NSA eavesdropping scandal. There is also an old saying that as long as someone knows a secret it is never safe. People can always divulge information, and odds are that they eventually will. There are many other ways to compromise verbal information.

Hardcopy information is any type of information that takes a physical form. It could be any printed document. It can also be a photograph. After all, as they say, "A picture is worth a thousand words." Sometimes physical samples of materials are also valuable. For example, a Japanese company had some of their employees dip their ties in a chemical sample of another company to get some to analyze. My friend, Stan, as a Soviet operative, was tasked with bringing back a sample of the coating around a Stealth Fighter. He was given a special pair of gloves that collected microscopic samples as he ran his hand over the fighter during a press conference.

I would also classify data storage, such as computer chips, data backup tapes, USB drives, and so on as hard copy information. While technically these devices contain information, the information on them is only physically vulnerable when not in a computer.

Electronic information takes on many forms. It could be any information on a computer, computer storage device, or data in transmission. E-mail is also a very vulnerable form of information. It is generally wide open and can be visible to hundreds of people around the world as it is transmitted. Likewise, there are also file and data transfers of all types going across the Internet and other computer networks. For example, credit card numbers are regularly traveling the Internet either through transactions or even through cash register terminals that connect to the payment clearing systems via such means.

The issue though is that if information is compromised, it doesn't matter how it was compromised. The loss is the same. For example, with theft of the Coca Cola secrets previously discussed, it actually didn't matter if the data was lost because the woman involved copied data off of a computer, made copies of a document, or stole a physical sample of the new drink. If the information is compromised, it is compromised.

When you create a security or risk mitigation program, you need to figure out what is valuable and all of the forms that the value can take. You have to protect it all, and you cannot shirk responsibility for ensuring such protection.

Let me end this chapter with one example of how a security program failed to look at all forms of information. The ChoicePoint scandal caused national headlines. Technically, nobody broke into their computers. What happened was criminals signed up for a valid merchant account, and ChoicePoint granted them the merchant account. As criminals, they accessed over 100,000 credit reports. ChoicePoint collected a fee from them for each credit report, and was happy to have them as a client. Of course, the criminals used the information in the credit reports to steal the identities of the people identified in the reports. ChoicePoint's computers did exactly what they were supposed to do. Is that a security success story?

Chapter 11

Is Security a
Should or a Must?

When I am asked as to whether security programs will succeed or fail, I always say that it depends on one thing: Does the person or organization believe that security is a *should* or a *must*?

Frankly, to most of the world, security is a should. While a few people and organizations don't care about security, most people believe that they should be secure. The key word is *should*. Should implies that if all other things were equal, they would choose to be secure. However, there is a clear difference between a should and a must. Someone who thinks that they *must* be secure will go to whatever lengths are required to achieve a reasonable security level.

The best way I know to address the difference between should and must is through the analogy of fitness. Think about a person who believes that fitness is a must. That person will always find a time and place to work out. They will eat healthy by default. They will pass up the dessert. They take the stairs instead of the elevator.

A person who thinks fitness is a should, and that is most people, will work out if it is convenient. While they want to work out in theory, there are many things that can and will come up that will get in their way of working out. They know they should pass up dessert, but a little never hurt anyone. Then they should stop at one bite, but they will just work out more the next day. Until of course something more important comes up.

You can always tell a person who believes that they must be fit. Their body reflects that attitude. Likewise, you know that there are times that they will not be available because they will be working out.

With people or organizations where security is a "should," it is a lot like dinnertime with a person who thinks fitness is a should. Well, we should stop people from having bad passwords, but we don't want them to have to write their passwords down. We should make people wear the badges all the time, but the dangling chains might be a safety hazard. We should put turnstiles with card readers in, but then we have to consider the disability laws. We could instead put guards by the doors, but that might be expensive, and people might be uncomfortable to see all those guards around.

I can contrast that with an organization that thought security is a must. To get on the corporate complex, you had to show a badge to the guards at gates to the corporate roadway. Then when you entered buildings, there were guards in the lobbies and mantrap turnstiles to get into the work areas. All rooms off of the hallways were closed and had crypto locks. While security was not perfect, it was exponentially more secure than most other corporations in the world.

Look at airline security for shoulds and musts. In the wake of the September 11th attacks, the air traffic controllers ordered all airplanes grounded. They did not know what was going on or the scope of the problem, so they thought the only way to stop future attacks was to get all planes on the ground. Security was a must. Today, passengers are screened, but commercial airlines are not, because it just seems logistically impractical. Likewise, less than 3 percent of freight brought into the United States is screened. Security is a should.

Must security does not mean that you strive for perfect security. It does imply that when you identify a vulnerability that you need to counter, you don't make excuses as to why the counter-measure isn't perfect for your organization. For example, time and time again I run into organizations where anyone can walk in or out of their buildings. I recommend that these companies limit entrances, and I hear everything from the fact that it might cause some inconvenience, the employees won't like it, they need smoking areas, it inhibits their environment of openness, and so on. In one company, it took an incident where a man walked into one of the doors I recommended be locked and he assaulted his girlfriend, to finally lock the doors.

When you believe security is a must, if a countermeasure cost effectively mitigates a vulnerability, it is implemented unless there are some incredibly compelling reasons not to implement it. You will always think of a reason not to implement something, but it doesn't mean that they are compelling.

When security is a should, I sit in a room telling the security staff what my recommendations are, and they sit there coming up with one reason after another as to why it might not work. I try to get them to acknowledge that those are potentially valid concerns and then focus on the counters to those concerns and why the countermeasures are more compelling than the arguments against them. The problem is that in organizations where security is a should, the security staff has been demoralized. They stop trying to focus on the right things as they know that they are fighting a losing battle.

When security is a must you will still have problems arise. However, the problems will be more contained and cause significantly less damage. You will be able to detect the problems more effectively, and you will have a process in place to respond to those problems. Probably more importantly, you may be able to detect incidents in their early phases, before any damage is caused. For example, when you check audit logs regularly, you can see someone performing reconnaissance for their attacks and stop them before they go further.

Management Must
Believe Security is a Must

Security needs to be a must throughout all levels of your organization to be successful. Clearly, though, it is more important to have executive support. When you have executive support the rest of the organization will follow.

Clearly, security is a grass roots activity. The Chief Executive Officer (CEO) is not going to take off the passwords taped to monitors, or personally ensure every door is locked. Therefore, the first line managers are actually the most important for ensuring that security policies and procedures are followed. Likewise, the physical security staff has to verify that physical security policies are followed as they do their rounds, and the information security staff has to verify that technical policies are being adhered to and enforced.

However, even the best-intentioned employees will slip up. Likewise, many employees are lazy and will purposefully ignore security policies and procedures. If the security staffs are not given the authority to enforce their rules, then the organization's security posture will quickly deteriorate.

In one organization I was in performing an espionage simulation, I literally stole billions of dollars of their information in a few hours. Throughout the whole test, I kept hearing that the researchers had to be kept happy so that they were productive. The good part of this is that the CEO finally realized that his researchers were potentially being productive for their competitors as well. More importantly, he realized that he could be personally liable for shareholder lawsuits if it was determined that the information was easily stolen by a competitor, causing their company to lose shareholder value.

The CEO then realized that he had to change the attitudes of his employees. He started to give the security staff the power to enforce the policies that they had in place. When it was demonstrated that consistent flaunting of security policies could result in dismissal, it was clear that security became a must.

As I previously stated, security staffs get demoralized when they are ignored. The reason is that the executive management has sent them a message that their job responsibilities are subordinate to other aspects of the business. Their job is relegated to fighting fires. They are basically given responsibility with no authority.

So is Security a Should or Must For You?

Frankly, the big issue is to either accept that you believe that is a should, or decide that security is a must. A must doesn't mean that there are no compromises, but it does mean that vulnerabilities are mitigated as appropriate. It does mean that the security staffs have the authority to go along with their responsibility, and that people are appropriately disciplined as rules are violated.

If you are not willing to accept security as a must, stop faking it. You are just deluding yourself to believe that you have some semblance of security. The fact is that you are being compromised on a regular basis. If that is the case, you have to create a security program that goes in that direction. You have to purposefully hire security personnel who don't care too much about their job. While this may sound counterintuitive, the fact is that a conscientious security professional will get frustrated and create internal tensions.

Likewise, if security is a must, you should hire the best staff that you can. Frankly, when you guarantee people that they will be completely supported, you will have people beating a path to your door.

Again, I can tell how secure an organization will be based upon the answer to a few questions from the management, employees, or security staff. When security is a should, people will tell you that security is secondary to business concerns. The security staff demonstrates a great deal of frustration. Employees have a casual attitude to security policies.

I want to be clear about one thing, though. When security is a must, it does not mean that security is a priority over business concerns. When security is a must, security is integrated into business concerns. It is a business concern.

Chapter 12

If You Don't Remember History, You Will Repeat It

I was recently asked to give a presentation about e-mail security. I was thinking about what to talk about, and I realized that no matter what I came up with, there was very little unique about e-mail security when compared with computer security as a whole. I ended up giving a presentation that someone referred to as the "History of the Internet."

When I thought about e-mail viruses and worms, they just seemed to be a different delivery mechanism than the Morris worm that came out in 1988. Likewise the Slammer, Blaster, Code Red, Nimda, Sasser (enter your favorite worm here), are all fundamentally identical in nature to the Morris worm.

This chapter came up as an afterthought when I started thinking about the fact that in 2003, the Information Systems Security Association did a study and found that 70 percent of their members have been in the security profession for less than 3 years. The importance of this ironically came up when I debated the notorious hacker Kevin Mitnick. Mitnick's self-tailored introduction painted him as a person who got caught up in his teenage transgressions, and was the victim of overzealous prosecution. During the debate, however, I pointed out that he was arrested and convicted five times and involved in the criminal justice system for over 20 years. There was a mumbling in the audience as they discussed the fact that Mitnick's criminal record was much larger than they thought.

Most security professionals do not realize that his latest claims of reformation are identical to those the last time he got out of jail in the early 1990s. After having no success being accepted as a security professional, he went on the run and committed a whole new set of felonies. The outrage that he was held without bail was over a moot issue in that they did not need to consider bail. He was guilty of probation violations, on top of the fact that he proved himself to be a flight risk. Still there are many security professionals who only know the hype and are willing to hire Mitnick, creating very significant potential liability for them and their organization.

Security professionals not familiar with the history of the industry will make decisions that allow history to repeat itself.

An old saying goes, "The more things change, the more they stay the same." That is definitely true with information security. I already discussed the fact that there are only two fundamental ways to hack a computer: take advantage of the vulnerabilities built into the software and take advantage in the way a computer is configured or maintained. Any attacks against computers happen that way. If you don't properly maintain your computers, you shouldn't be surprised that they are compromised.

Think about all the Internet-based scams that are out there. There is nothing new about them. For example, there is the common, "I am the son of a dead dictator, and I need help laundering money," scam. While people want to attribute this to the Internet, these scams were faxed to people before the Internet. Before faxes, people would mail letters. The scam is nothing new, but people want to believe it is for some reason. The Internet just makes it more common.

Another common Internet scam is fake lotteries. Criminals spam people with claims that they have won a multimillion-dollar lottery, and then want money to pay the taxes to clear the money. Before the Internet, people would create fake lottery tickets and then make up some excuse as to why they didn't want to claim the money themselves. Of course the lottery tickets would look like unclaimed winning lottery tickets. The "victims" are asked to pay a small part of the value of the ticket, and then they themselves can claim the winnings in their name.

Even when you look at the extreme example of the September 11th attacks, there was nothing new about those attacks. Suicide bombers were previously combined with many modes of transportation. There were the truck bomb attacks on US embassies, as well as on the Marine barracks in Lebanon. There was the bombing of the USS Cole using a boat. Why then would airplanes be considered a surprise? After all, terrorists have been hijacking airplanes for decades, and the FBI even arrested Zacarius Moussaui, with documents stating to the effect that he seemed to want to fly airplanes into buildings.

History can be used to predict economic trends, politics, and so many other aspects of our lives. There is not one element of our lives where history cannot be applied to understand how our current circumstances will progress.

There are so many lessons that history has for us. Sometimes there is a little modification or creativity added to past events; however, that doesn't justify pleading ignorance when something does happen. No matter what people want to believe, computers aren't creating any new security scams. They are just evolving old scams.

There are some attacks that are new and completely novel; however, they are so few and far between that it is ridiculous to believe that what you are facing with regard to security issues cannot be helped by looking into past events. This is true for both a macro and a micro level.

Appendix A lists significant events in information security history. These are definitely not intended to be all encompassing. They try to show enough events for effect to demonstrate that there are few revolutionary attacks that you need to face.

Computers have clearly enhanced the ability of criminals to reach a targeted audience. Computers have also clearly increased the scope of what is at risk, given that electronic assets can be copied in a second and the assailant can be more than 10,000 miles away. This clearly increases the risk that you have to deal with. Again, though, the attacks themselves are nothing new, and this allows you to protect yourself more effectively, or at least points you to how to mitigate your damages.

Chapter 13

Ira's Golden Rules

There are plenty of things you can do to secure your organization. As I said, some of the security countermeasures are a waste. However, many can be very valuable to your organization. There are, however, some things that are clear security musts, whether you are an individual or a Fortune 500 company.

As I close this book, it is best that I close with information that everyone can immediately apply. Throughout the book, I have focused on information that helps people think about security and all of the myths that they face. I personally believe that this information is infinitely more useful than any mechanical application of an individual security control.

However, there are some universal security countermeasures that you need to implement, again whether you are an individual or a Fortune 500 company. Without these issues, you are leaving yourself widely vulnerable to trivial attacks. By this time, you should realize that while it is always possible that you will be successfully attacked, it is inexcusable to leave yourself open to a completely preventable attack.

The following are my golden rules for information security.

Take Responsibility

This is the most important rule of all. You need to accept responsibility for what you have control of. If you only have a PC, accept that you are responsible for what happens on that PC. If you provide network access, accept that you are responsible for what goes across the network. If you maintain servers, accept that you are responsible for the security of the systems, and most importantly the data on those systems.

It is sad to think that I have to actually state this. Unfortunately though, when something goes wrong, people love to blame the assailant, their vendors, their customers, whomever. Maybe other people are at fault for the attack itself. However, that is going to do you no good at all if you have a loss. You have to acknowledge that you must do what you can to proactively protect yourself and respond to any incidents.

Likewise, if you are in business providing a service, you need to proactively take responsibility for what you can. For example, I advocate that Internet Service Providers (ISPs) stop attack traffic that passes through their networks. While the ISPs might not be directly affected by attacks that pass through their network pipes, they have to constantly increase their equipment to handle the increased volumes of data involved in the attacks. There is an effect for everyone in the chain of an attack.

Decide Security is a Must

As I said in a previous chapter, many people treat security as a *should* and not a *must*. You must decide that security is a business concern, and not something that is nice to have if you can fit it in. Security must be considered a part of all operations.

For example, a credit card processor must state that their business is providing secure processing of credit card transactions, not processing of credit card transactions. Your home computer is to provide safe computing for your family's needs, not provide computing for your family's needs.

Again, I am not saying that security is the top priority. Security must be integrated into the overall requirements of information. Security is really providing risk management, and risk management must be a consideration in the handling of any information. It must not be an after thought or something to be incorporated if time or money allows.

Think of it this way. When you send a child to school, you generally make sure that they are dressed appropriately for the weather. You cannot be a good parent by alone stating that you sent your child to school. You would be declared negligent if you sent your child to school with shorts and a t-shirt during a snow-storm. The clothing is an integral security measure. When you use information or computers, you need to make sure they are secured appropriately for their environment as well.

Educate Yourself

Probably the most critical aspect of taking responsibility is that you need to develop your common knowledge. If you have children, you have to learn about the technologies that they use. If you don't know what pos, wtgp, and mip mean, you better learn.

If a child can learn about this, so can you. If you cannot, you should have yourself committed. You would be either lazy or stupid. There is nothing that inherently enables children to understand technology that adults cannot.

Gathering common knowledge helps to steer you away from malicious Web sites and other cases of Internet fraud. A lack of knowledge can be addressed. It must be addressed.

Remember, You are Protecting Information

As I said before, you are not protecting computers, you are protecting the information and services offered by the computers. This not only implies that your computers have more value than the price tag, but that your conversations and maybe even crumbled up pieces of paper have immense value as well.

I don't know how many times I have sat on a flight and the person next to me is doing their monthly bills or preparing a business expense report. Both ways, I see their credit card numbers. Likewise, I listen to people on their cell phones buying something and can hear their credit card numbers as well. This is just a single example of how innocuous actions can lead to major losses.

Not only do you need to protect your computers, you need to shred potentially sensitive information that is printed. You need to consider who can potentially hear your conversations about the information, or look over your shoulder as you read the information. Just as ChoicePoint likely protected consumer credit records on their computers, they needed to make sure that they didn't sell the credit records to criminals. You need to look at how information is used and protect it in all of its forms.

Protecting Your Computer

While I like to think of this book as much more than a computer security book, I know for a fact that it will be placed in the computer security section of the bookstore. I also know that if a computer security professional buys this book, it will be proverbially preaching to the choir. However, I hope that more than experienced computer security professionals will be reading this book and will benefit from these suggestions. Maybe computer security professionals can at least use this section to prove that their recommendations are important.

Another thing I want to stress for this section is that many people initially have all of the countermeasures that I advocate, but they let the related software expire or they just stop doing the right things. Hopefully, people will either implement or renew these countermeasures as appropriate.

Use and Renew Anti-Virus Software

The most common computer-related attacks are viruses. One scumbag after another is trying to write new viruses or modifying known viruses all the time. When a virus hits, the effects can be devastating, potentially causing the loss of millions of dollars of work or destroying years' worth of pictures and memories.

All Windows-based PCs and Macs need to run anti-virus software. Despite the very misleading Mac commercials, there are Mac viruses out there. The only reason that there are more PC-based viruses is that there are significantly fewer Mac users, so attackers don't care about Macs enough to attack them frequently.

Most importantly, you need to make sure that your anti-virus software is configured to automatically update itself. Just think of it as letting a car fill up its fuel tank on its own. Anti-virus software can update itself daily or more frequently if required by fast spreading attacks.

One place where people fail is when users do not renew their anti-virus software licenses. Yes, this can be upwards of $50 per year, but again it is required maintenance, just like it is required that you change the oil of your car. The anti-virus software might apparently work properly, however, you will not get the updates for the new viruses. You might not like it, but it is a required cost of owning a computer.

Use and Renew Personal Firewalls

Anti-virus software does not stop all attacks against a computer. Viruses are essentially computer programs that are placed on your computer to perform bad actions. There are attacks that target the software that runs on your computer. As previously described, this software can either be misconfigured or have vulnerabilities built into it. Personal firewalls intend to prevent remote threats from exploiting those vulnerabilities, among others.

This software must be installed on PCs. It doesn't matter whether or not you have a firewall built into some router that connects your house to your ISP. Those router/firewalls prevent a

Ira's Golden Rules 禅 Chapter 13

large number of attacks but not everything. Laptops that can connect anywhere are definitely susceptible as well.

Exactly as is the case with anti-virus software, personal firewall software should be configured to automatically update itself. Additionally, as with the case of anti-virus software, you need to renew the license annually. On a good note, personal firewall software is available for purchase as a security software suite.

Use and Renew Anti-Spyware

While some anti-virus programs detect some forms of spyware, they do not intend to or proclaim that they are anti-spyware programs. While I personally believe the only difference between viruses and spyware is the damage they cause, I really don't know why it is different. Sadly, this is irrelevant as you have to accept reality and take responsibility for protecting your information. To fully do that, you must have anti-spyware software on your PCs.

Again, anti-spyware needs to be allowed to update itself, as well as renewed annually. Anti-spyware is frequently bundled with security software suites.

With anti-spyware, I actually recommend that people install two different anti-spyware products. The reason is that the quality of different anti-spyware products varies. No individual product appears to catch everything. As I was writing this book, I had a top-rated security suite anti-spyware product running on my system. I thought one of my computers was running a little off, so I ran another anti-spyware product and found three low-level, spyware infections.

As I mentioned, you can buy anti-spyware in a security suite to satisfy one of your needs, and keep it always running. The other anti-spyware product should be a standalone product, and you can run it once a week; more frequently, if you notice that you have problems.

135

Run Weekly Backups

As I keep repeating, even if you do everything right, you will likely have problems. Even if you never have a virus, your hard drive might crash. Something can always go wrong. For that reason, you should perform at least a weekly backup of your sensitive files. You don't have to back up the whole computer, as most of the data on the computer is applications or operating systems software. You only need to back up the information that you create or modify on the system.

For example, you don't need to backup your e-mail reader, but you do need to backup the e-mail itself. You don't need to backup your word processing software, but you do need to backup the documents you create. Windows computers make it relatively easy to do this by having the *My Documents* directory. If you maintain your files in that directory, all you would have to do is backup that directory.

Most people can buy a Universal Serial Bus (USB) thumb drive that should be able to backup the whole *My Documents* directory. If someone has music or videos on their system, they might place all of those files in the *My Music* or *My Videos* directories, respectively. These would likely require more space than a typical thumb drive and could be backed up on CDs or external hard drives.

The key thing is to backup the data on a regular basis. While the title of this section recommends weekly backups, if you have very valuable information that changes frequently, you should back it up daily.

Use Uninterruptible Power Supplies

One of the most damaging things that can happen to a computer is a sudden power loss or power surge. At the very least, a power loss will cause a loss of recent data changes. It can also cause hard drive crashes, which can cause you to lose all data on the drive. A power surge is a sudden increase in power going into your computer. This can happen for a variety of reasons, including lightning strikes in the area. A power surge can destroy electronic devices.

Uninterruptible Power Supplies (UPS) are basically big batteries. You plug the UPS into the power outlet, and then plug your computer into the UPS. If there is a power loss, the battery backup feature kicks in, and provides you with enough time to save your work and properly shut down the computer. Some UPSes connect directly to the computer, and will work with the computer to automatically shut it down if unattended. There are different sizes of UPSes that provide varying amounts of battery backup time.

UPS also provide surge protection. It is not practical or necessary to use a UPS for all devices. In those cases, you can buy special power strips with surge protection. It should also be noted that power surges can also go through telephone lines. Many surge protectors include outlets for telephone lines as well, and you should utilize them.

Note on Security Software

I consider the security software products I mention in this chapter to be critical and required. However, I acknowledge that running all of the software can cause it to run very slowly. I myself have been periodically tempted to disable my software. However, that is unacceptable to me.

You can deactivate the anti-spyware and manually run it on a daily basis. The big processing hog is usually the anti-virus software. One thing you can do to minimize the processing drain is to deactivate the e-mail scanning during sending e-mails.

Short of the above, another solution is to try different security products. That can, however, appear to waste money. If your computer is more than three years old, you can try to either upgrade the computer with additional random-access memory (RAM) or a faster processor, or just buy a new computer.

Again, security is not a driving issue, but it is an integral issue. If you cannot adequately protect yourself while you are connected to the outside world, you should not do it. There is a lot to lose.

The 95/5 Rule

While this chapter has very critical advice, it is only a start in securing your personal or your organization's information. This is the 95/5 rule in my opinion. The 80/20 rule implies that you can solve 80 percent of your problems with 20 percent of the effort. I think my golden rules provide you with 95/5; 5 percent of the effort can solve 95 percent of your information security problems.

There is still, however, the 5 percent that you have to deal with. That last 5 percent can be very difficult to handle, but you are at least taking care of the proverbial low-hanging fruit that even the most inept script kiddie will be able to grab.

Chapter 14

Chance Favors
the Prepared

One day, my computer was running slow as I was clearing out my spam folder. What happens is, it is possible that you might intend to click on one function and you actually end up clicking something else. In this case, I accidentally opened up an e-mail with a malicious executable. As I saw my hard drive start to spin, I cringed and then attempted to pull out the Ethernet cable to try to stop some potential effects of what was clearly malicious software.

After a few seconds, I was incredibly relieved as a pop-up window appeared on my screen from my anti-virus software. The window said that a virus was detected and that it was deleted. While my click was clearly an accident, it really doesn't matter. These things happen, and accidents should be expected. You really can't anticipate every type of accident; however, by taking all reasonable risk management steps, you can proactively mitigate the damaging effects of most accidents, and even most malicious acts. As I described it before, preparation helps to mitigate the damages of both malicious and malignant threats.

It was not luck that I had anti-virus software installed, updated, and continuously running. It is accidents like this that show me why I always need anti-virus software, even though it slows down my computer. As I said, anti-virus and other security software is a must with regard to being proactively secure.

Ubiquitous Security

Throughout this book, I have used the automobile analogy. Again, a car is a very complicated piece of equipment, more complicated than a computer. There are millions of people who can potentially cause you harm on the roads. Despite this, people are still comfortable driving cars and generally make it through the day.

The reason is that there is an infrastructure in place to prevent harm. There are safety devices embedded in the car. People need to pass a basic skills test to get a driver's license. Roads are kept in good repair, and cars are required to be kept in good repair. There are street signs and signals to control the flow of traffic. Traffic laws also state how drivers are required to behave. There is enforcement of laws. Security is ubiquitous to driving.

The tools and techniques required to prevent just about all attacks, is available to us now. The knowledge is available. However, people have been unwilling to apply the tools, knowledge, and techniques, leaving themselves vulnerable to even the most trivial attack.

I already mentioned my *Wizard of Oz* analogy. If people used what they already have, we could make very significant increases in our security. Security would be ubiquitous to computers and information as a whole.

The Purpose of This Book

Frankly, if you are reading this I am honored. Most people generally don't finish books, primarily because they lose interest. Even if readers believe that the information is valuable, they might get lazy or get too busy. While I still attribute that to the fact that I am not able to compel the reader enough to continue for any reason, I have to accept this as a condition of being an author.

As I close I feel I should drive home the point that security is driven by how you think, not any technologies. Technologies are the implementation of your thought processes. If you have bad thought processes, you will have bad security. It is that simple.

I should specify that it might not be you as an individual who has the bad thought processes. I have met many very competent security professionals who think the right way. Unfortunately, their management doesn't support what they want to do, so the organization as a whole doesn't think the right way. Again, it is my hope that this book might assist these people in helping get management to support their security staff.

Technology is Still Important

I fully admit that I downplay the role of technology and the many complicated aspects of implementing good computer and information security. There is definitely a need for many of the great tools that are available. It is therefore critical that as I recommend, you go out and get educated on what you need to know. Ignorance is no excuse for a parent, and it is no excuse for anyone who uses computers or information.

I strongly recommend that you go out and read books on the technologies and subjects that are relevant to you or your organization. There is a tremendous amount of information out there that addresses just about any security concern that you may have. Ignorance is unjustifiable.

Security is Really Risk Management

Again, you can never be secure. It is a fictional state. You will never be without risk of loss in one way or another. As the reactions to the 9/11 attacks demonstrated, the only way you can prevent airline hijackings is to stop airline flights. That is not a realistic situation. Ironically, more people probably died while taking long road trips while the airplanes were grounded as a result of the action.

If you are in the real world, you have to acknowledge that loss will happen. Your goal is to cost effectively control that loss. Most importantly, you cannot just say that no matter what you do, there will be loss, so why try?

This is a despicable attitude that too many companies and individuals have. Even worse is the attitude that information technology is too complicated to understand, so why bother? This leaves people ignorant about something that is ubiquitous to daily life. This is the technological equivalent of walking around a crime ridden neighborhood asking, "Where is a bank where I can deposit $100,000 in cash?"

Every individual and organization needs to identify the relevant threats, vulnerabilities, and value that they have, so that they can determine the countermeasures that they need. Those countermeasures are not intended to eliminate all loss, but to cost effectively mitigate as much loss as reasonable.

Be Responsible

The way I want to end this book is by reminding people that they need to accept responsibility for what they have control over. A thief might target you, but that doesn't mean that you make it easy for the thief. It doesn't mean that you take no measures to stop the thief.

If you are a parent, you need to learn about the technology your children use. You need to learn about how they use the technology. You also need to accept the responsibility that if your child sneaks out of the house to meet someone, how they met the person is the least irrelevant compared to the fact that your child's care and behavior is your responsibility. Learn how to spy on your kids. They are good at spying on you.

You should also assume responsibility for the fact that your actions can affect others. Given the nature of the Internet and the value of information, if you leave a computer or information, in any form, vulnerable, you are facilitating harm on other people. To me that is worse than just leaving yourself or your own organization vulnerable. While many people love to disparage lawyers, I look forward to widespread lawsuits against companies who left information grossly unprotected. Sadly, it will take something like this to make security a must for most people.

There are a lot of different things in the world that may cause you harm. Clearly, you cannot, nor is it reasonable to expect that you can, protect yourself or your organization from everything. You are expected, though, to take reasonable precautions, to reasonably manage your risk. Just like Dorothy had her ruby red slippers throughout most of *The Wizard of Oz*, you have what you need, or you can get it. You just need to acknowledge your responsibility to use the information and technologies.

Appendix A

Critical Moments
in Computer
Security History

The list below indicates some of the major events in computer security history. This list is definitely not all encompassing, but intends to show that just about all attacks that we see today, and will see in the future, are only variants of attacks that we have seen for decades. This information is only demonstrative in nature.

For a more detailed listing of events, you can search Wikipedia and other Internet sources. There is no single listing that appears to be all encompassing.

1971	John Draper invents the first Blue Box, providing people a method to make free telephone calls
Early 1970s	The Creeper virus is detected on the ARPAnet, which is the early version of the Internet.
1978	The term "Hacker" is first attributed to teenage computer criminals, who hack the telephone system, misdirecting telephone calls and listening into in on conversations Computer bulletin board systems provide for hacker exchange of information
1981	The first widespread virus was released. Elk Cloner targeted early Apple computers.
1983	The movie, War Games, comes out and glamorizes teenage hacking. Demonstrates the use of vulnerability of open modems and guessable passwords.
1984	The magazine, 2600, begins publishing and makes hacking information available to people who aren't familiar with computers.

1986	Computer Fraud and Abuse Act, a.k.a 1030, goes into effect, formerly making unauthorized access to computers a crime.
1988	The Morris Worm is released into the wild. It targeted vulnerabilities in certain versions of the UNIX operating system. It temporarily crippled approximately one third of what was considered the Internet at the time.
1988	First significant acknowledgement of a large computer crime against a bank. $70,000,000 loss was experienced by First National Bank of Chicago due to computer crime.
1989	The Cuckoo's Egg incident becomes public. Cliff Stoll, a systems administrator for Lawrence Livermore National Labs, notices and investigates hacking of defense defense-related systems and tracks the incident back to computer hackers in West Germany, hacking on behalf of the KGB. The case demonstrates the vulnerability of defense defense-related information and the targeting of such information by foreign intelligence services.
1990	The AT&T long distance telephone system crashed in the US Northeast. While computer hackers were originally suspected in the incident, it was soon determined to be the result of a 3 line programming error in their switching system software.
	The Secret Service launches Operation Sundevil, which targeted hacker BBS that facilitated the trading of credit cards and information about compromising telephone systems.

1991	The Michelangelo virus gains notoriety for computer viruses in the minds of the general public.
1992	The movie, "Sneakers," is released, popularizing the concept of penetration testing.
1994	Hackers move hacking BBSes to web Web-based forums
	Authorities arrest Vladmir Levin for hacking into Citibank electronic funds transfer systems, stealing upwards of $10,000,000. All but $400,000 was recovered.
1995	US Government report states that there are over 250,000 attacks against Department of Defense (DoD) computers.
Mid 1990s	DoD performs Eligible Receiver exercises, simulating hostile computer actions against US government and military assets. The US government and military are deemed widely vulnerable to attack through known vulnerabilities.
1998	Operation Solar Sunrise attempts to locate perpetrators of "The most coordinated and sophisticated attacks" experienced by the DoD. Attackers are discovered to be two script kiddies.
1999	Melissa worm causes billions of dollars of damage.
2000	Hacker attempts to extort CD Universe by threatening to release customer information unless paid $100,000.

I Love You virus is released. This is the first large scale virus that used Social Engineering techniques.

Massive Distributed Denial of Service (DDOS) attacks target Amazon, CNN, Yahoo!, and other companies. The attack was attributed to a Canadian teenager. The attacks demonstrate the dangers of botnets.

| 2001 | Code Red worm targets known vulnerabilities and creates billions of dollars of damager around the world. |

Nimda worm targets similar vulnerabilities to Code Red, and is initially thought to be terrorist terrorist-related due to its release soon after the September 11th attacks.

| 2002 | After an embarrassing security vulnerability, Microsoft performs a programming stand down to provide security security-related training to all developers. |

| 2003 | Slammer worm targets Microsoft SQL servers and wreaks havoc on computer networks around the world. |

Despite widespread media coverage of the importance of patching the underlying problem, the Blaster worm is released to the wild and causes billions of dollars of damage.

| 2004 | Sasser worm spreads quickly, creating billions of dollars in damages. |

2005	Paris Hilton's cell phone account is hacked through Social Engineering of a T-Mobile store's employee. The resulting publicity generates a public spectacle and demonstrates the danger of storing information on cell phones.

Index

A

Abene, Mark, 108

ability, factor affecting qualities of scientists, 18–19

adversaries and competitors, 102–104

airline security, 117

al Qaeda, 65, 70

anthrax as threat, vs. Nimba worm, 77–78

anti-spyware, 141

anti-virus software, 139–140, 143, 146

application programs, vulnerabilities of, 55–56

art of security vs. science of security, 16–18

attacks

  on Department of Defense computers, 66–67

  hackers, categories of, 69–71

  ISPs blocking, 137

  number of preventable, 61

  phishing, 83

  SQL injection, 56

audit logs, 118

B

backing up information, 142

bin Laden, Osama, 64, 65, 71

black belt, martial arts, 52–54

Black Duck Eggs, 10–11

book, purpose of this, 147–148

budgets

  costs and considerations, 44–47

  multiyear, 48

bugs

  finding, fixing, 57–59

  software-related vulnerabilities, 56

Bush, George W., 64

C

Charney, Scott, 100, 107

Cheney, Dick, 33

Chief Information Officer (CIO), duties of, 47

children, computer competence of, 109–110

ChoicePoint scandal, 114

CIA, and Valerie Plame scandal, 326–33

Clarke, Richard, 66
click fraud, 70
Clinton, Bill, 65
Code Red worm, 77–78
competitor value, 28–29
competitors and adversaries, 102
Computer Emergency Response Team (CERT), bug-created vulnerabilities, 55
computer geniuses, 69–70
computer hackers, 17, 69–71
computers
  anti-virus software on, 139–140
  backing up, 142
  personal firewalls, 140–141
  securing, 60–61
  updates and maintenance, 86–89
  ways of hacking, 54–61
configuration errors
  and bad passwords, 59
  and vulnerabilities, 60–61
Corporate Espionage, 106
costs
  and benefits of IT security, 83–86

of resetting passwords, 40–41
countermeasures
  budgeting, 46–47
  implementing, 118
  and security, 34–36
credit card fraud, 92–93, 138–139
criminals
  mindset of, 106–110
  organized crime, 103–104
  stupidity and incompetence of, 91–98
cybercriminals, 104–105
cyberterrorism
  professional hackers, 70
  threat of, 76–77

D

Dateline's To Catch a Predator, 95
Department of Defense
  Eligible Receiver exercises, 23–24
  hack of computers, 107
  Operation Solar Sunrise, 66
Department of Homeland Security, train hazardous material markings, 30

disaster recovery, hurricanes, 35–36, 72–73

Dive Master, 50–53

'dragons'
  and FUD factor, 65–66
  and 'knights,' 64–67
  vs. 'snakes,' 71

E

e-mail
  backing up, 142
  deactivating anti-spyware scanning, 143
  security, 130

eBay, fraud on, 88

enemies
  and adversaries, 99
  'dragons' and 'knights,' 64–67
  hackers, categories of, 69–71
  and the philosophy of security, 12–14

F

FaceBook, 110

factors affecting qualities of scientists, 18–22

fake lotteries, 131

fear, uncertainly, and doubt (FUD) factor, 65–66, 77, 79

firewalls
  and administrator errors, 60–61
  using, 140–141

foreign intelligence agencies, 103

formula, risk, 26

fraud, credit card, 92–93, 138–139

FTC (Federal Trade Commission), and cybercrime prosecutions, 84

FUD (fear, uncertainly, and doubt) factor, 65–66, 77, 79

G

Gaede, William, 106

goals of security programs, 36

H

hackers
  categories of, 69–71
  described, 17

hacking
    computers, ways to, 54–61
    information available on
        Web, 21–22
Hayden, Lance, 109
Hewlett Packard (HP)
    scandal, 97–98
hurricanes, 35–36, 72–73

I

identity theft, 83, 99–100
information
    backing up, 142
    securing, 112–114
    security, 138
Information Resources
    Management (IRM), 47
infrastructure
    security, 46, 146–147
    as terrorist target, 78
insider adversaries, 100–101
insurance, and optimizing
    risk, 37
Internet
    ISP security, 84
    terrorist uses of, 76
    warez sites, 93
IRM (Information Resources
    Management), 47

ISPs (Internet Service
    Providers)
    blocking attack traffic, 137
    security of, 84
IT security
    cost of, 44–47
    costs and benefits of, 83–86
    determining budget of,
        47–48
    prioritization of, 116–121

J

Jordon, Michael, 19
Judge Judy, 86

K

Kenpo Masters, 54
'knights' and 'dragons,' 64–67

L

Libby, 'Scooter,' 33
lotteries, fake, 131

M

Macintosh
    security vulnerabilities of,
        57
    viruses on, 140
Madrid subway bombings, 77

malicious, malignant threats, 29–31

management, presenting security budget to, 48–49

managing loss or risk, 26

master described, 52–54

McFee Site Advisor, 88

MICE (money, ideology, coercion, and ego), 101–102

Microsoft, software vulnerabilities of products, 57

Microsoft Update Service, 57

Mitnick, Kevin, 100, 130–131

monetary value, 28

money, ideology, coercion, and ego (MICE), 101–102

multiyear IT security budgets, 48

MySpace.com, 30, 110

N

Nimba worm, 77–78

NIST, NSA Web sites, system hardening documents, 61

nuisance value, 28

O

operating systems vulnerabilities, 55
  Windows/Vista, 57

Operation Solar Sunrise, 66

operational vulnerabilities, 32–33

operations, security and, 13–14

opportunist hackers, 71

optimizing risk, 37–42

organized crime, 103–104

P

passwords
  forgotten, cost of resetting, 40–41
  using secure, 59
  weak, 82
  Windows 95 vulnerability, 56

patches, security, 57

penetration testing, 12, 108

personal firewalls, 140–141

personnel countermeasures, 34

personnel vulnerabilities, 33

philosophy of security, 13–14

phishing attacks, 83

physical countermeasures, 34

physical vulnerabilities, 32

Plame, Valerie, 33

power supplies, uninterruptible, 142–143

practice, factor affecting qualities of scientists, 19–20

preventing configuration vulnerabilities, 61

prioritization of IT security, 116–121

professional hackers, 70

programs, computer
 See also specific program
 built-in vulnerabilities, 55–56
 script kiddies, 71

programs, security, 36

Q

quality science, factors affecting, 18–22

R

Reagan, Ronald, 64

renewing anti-spyware, 141

resetting passwords, cost of, 40–41

return on investment (ROI) and security budget, 47

risk
 consciously accepting, 41, 49
 formula, 26
 management, 137
 optimizing, 37–41
 and security, 26–27

ROI (return on investment) and security budget, 47

S

science
 factors affecting qualities of scientists, 18–22
 of security, 16–18

script kiddies, 71, 94–95, 105–106

securing your information, 112–114

security
 95/5 rule, 144
 airline, 117
 art vs. science, 16–18
 audit logs, 118
 countermeasures and, 34–36
 defined, 26

determining IT security, 47–48

mastering computer, 54–62

patches, 57

philosophy of, 13–14

policies, unenforced, 85

prioritizing, 116–121

programs described, 36

risk and, 26–27

taking responsibility for, 136–137, 149

threat and, 29–31

value and, 27–29

vulnerabilities and, 31–33

of your information, 112–114

September 11 attacks and FUD factor, 65–66

simulations, espionage, 23

social engineering, 8, 9

software

anti-virus, 139–140, 143, 146

built-in vulnerabilities, 55–56

finding, fixing bugs, 58–59

Spies Among Us, 68

spyware, anti-spyware, 141

SQL injection attacks, 56

Structured Query Language (SQL) injection attacks, 56

stupidity

and common sense, 86–87

and the criminal mind, 107

suicide bombers, 132

surge protectors, 143

T

technical countermeasures, 34

technical vulnerabilities, 32

techniques, amateur hackers', 17

terrorists

competence of, 67–68

and FUD factor, 79

and malicious threats, 30

and professional hackers, 70

suicide bombers, 132

testing for visualization, 19–20

threats

cyberterrorism, 76–77

insider adversaries, 100–101

and security, 29–31

thumb drives for backup, 142

training, quality of, 18

U

uninterruptible power supplies (UPS), 142–143
updates, Windows Update Service, 88
USB (Universal Serial Bus) thumb drives, 142

V

value
  of IT security, 45–47
  and risk, 26–29
viruses, anti-virus software, 139–140
visualization, testing for, 19–20
vulnerabilities
  determining for budget, 47
  finding, fixing software, 58–59
  and risk optimization, 40–41
  and security, 31–33

W

warez sites, 93
warfare and terrorism, 77

Web pages
  See also Internet
  hacking information on, 21
'what' threats, 31
'who' threats, 29, 30–31
Windows 95 password vulnerability, 54–56
Windows Update Service, running automatically, 88
Windows/Vista operating systems, 56
Wizard of Oz, 87
worms, Nimba, Code Red, 77–78

Z

Zarqawi, 64
Zen and the Art of Motorcycle Maintenance (Pirsig), 16

Syngress: *The Definition of a Serious Security Library*

Syn•gress (sin–gres): *noun, sing.* Freedom from risk or danger; safety. See *security*.

Syngress: *The Definition of a Serious Security Library*

Syn•gress (sin–gres): *noun, sing.* Freedom from risk or danger; safety. See *security.*

Cyber Spying: Tracking Your Family's (Sometimes) Secret Online Lives

Dr. Eric Cole, Michael Nordfelt, Sandra Ring, and Ted Fair

Have you ever wondered about that friend your spouse e-mails, or who they spend hours chatting online with? Are you curious about what your children are doing online, whom they meet, and what they talk about? Do you worry about them finding drugs and other illegal items online, and wonder what they look at? This book shows you how to monitor and analyze your family's online behavior.

ISBN: 1-93183-641-8

Price: $39.95 US $57.95 CAN

Stealing the Network: How to Own an Identity

Timothy Mullen, Ryan Russell, Riley (Caezar) Eller, Jeff Moss, Jay Beale, Johnny Long, Chris Hurley, Tom Parker, Brian Hatch
The first two books in this series "Stealing the Network: How to Own the Box" and "Stealing the Network: How to Own a Continent" have become classics in the Hacker and Infosec communities because of their chillingly realistic depictions of criminal hacking techniques. In this third installment, the all-star cast of authors tackle one of the fastest-growing crimes in the world: Identity Theft. Now, the criminal hackers readers have grown to both love and hate try to cover their tracks and vanish into thin air…

ISBN: 1-59749-006-7

Price: $39.95 US $55.95 CAN

Software Piracy Exposed

Paul Craig, Ron Honick

For every $2 worth of software purchased legally, $1 worth of software is pirated illegally. For the first time ever, the dark underground of how software is stolen and traded over the Internet is revealed. The technical detail provided will open the eyes of software users and manufacturers worldwide! This book is a tell-it-like-it-is exposé of how tens of billions of dollars worth of software is stolen every year.

ISBN: 1-93226-698-4

Price: $39.95 U.S. $55.95 CAN

SYNGRESS®

Syngress: *The Definition of a Serious Security Library*

Syn·gress (sin-gres): *noun, sing.* Freedom from risk or danger; safety. See *security*.

Phishing Exposed

Lance James, Secure Science Corporation,
Joe Stewart (Foreword)

If you have ever received a phish, become a victim of a phish, or manage the security of a major e-commerce or financial site, then you need to read this book. The author of this book delivers the unconcealed techniques of phishers including their evolving patterns, and how to gain the upper hand against the ever-accelerating attacks they deploy. Filled with elaborate and unprecedented forensics, Phishing Exposed details techniques that system administrators, law enforcement, and fraud investigators can exercise and learn more about their attacker and their specific attack methods, enabling risk mitigation in many cases before the attack occurs.

ISBN: 1-59749-030-X

Price: $49.95 US $69.95 CAN

Penetration Tester's Open Source Toolkit

Johnny Long, Chris Hurley, SensePost,
Mark Wolfgang, Mike Petruzzi

This is the first fully integrated Penetration Testing book and bootable Linux CD containing the "Auditor Security Collection," which includes over 300 of the most effective and commonly used open source attack and penetration testing tools. This powerful tool kit and authoritative reference is written by the security industry's foremost penetration testers including HD Moore, Jay Beale, and SensePost. This unique package provides you with a completely portable and bootable Linux attack distribution and authoritative reference to the toolset included and the required methodology.

ISBN: 1-59749-021-0

Price: $59.95 US $83.95 CAN

Google Hacking for Penetration Testers

Johnny Long, Foreword by Ed Skoudis

Google has been a strong force in Internet culture since its 1998 upstart. Since then, the engine has evolved from a simple search instrument to an innovative authority of information. As the sophistication of Google grows, so do the hacking hazards that the engine entertains. Approaches to hacking are forever changing, and this book covers the risks and precautions that administrators need to be aware of during this explosive phase of Google Hacking.

ISBN: 1-93183-636-1

Price: $44.95 U.S. $65.95 CAN

SYNGRESS®

Syngress: *The Definition of a Serious Security Library*

Syn·gress (sin–gres): *noun, sing.* Freedom from risk or danger; safety. See *security.*

Cisco PIX Firewalls: Configure, Manage, & Troubleshoot

Charles Riley, Umer Khan, Michael Sweeney

Cisco PIX Firewall is the world's most used network firewall, protecting internal networks from unwanted intrusions and attacks. Virtual Private Networks (VPNs) are the means by which authorized users are allowed through PIX Firewalls. Network engineers and security specialists must constantly balance the need for air-tight security (Firewalls) with the need for on-demand access (VPNs). In this book, Umer Khan, author of the #1 best selling PIX Firewall book, provides a concise, to-the-point blueprint for fully integrating these two essential pieces of any enterprise network.

ISBN: 1-59749-004-0

Price: $49.95 US $69.95 CAN

Configuring Netscreen Firewalls

Rob Cameron

Configuring NetScreen Firewalls is the first book to deliver an in-depth look at the NetScreen firewall product line. It covers all of the aspects of the NetScreen product line from the SOHO devices to the Enterprise NetScreen firewalls. Advanced troubleshooting techniques and the NetScreen Security Manager are also covered..

ISBN: 1--93226-639-9

Price: $49.95 US $72.95 CAN

Configuring Check Point NGX VPN-1/FireWall-1

Barry J. Stiefel, Simon Desmeules

Configuring Check Point NGX VPN-1/Firewall-1 is the perfect reference for anyone migrating from earlier versions of Check Point's flagship firewall/VPN product as well as those deploying VPN-1/Firewall-1 for the first time. NGX includes dramatic changes and new, enhanced features to secure the integrity of your network's data, communications, and applications from the plethora of blended threats that can breach your security through your network perimeter, Web access, and increasingly common internal threats.

ISBN: 1--59749-031-8

Price: $49.95 U.S. $69.95 CAN

SYNGRESS®

Syngress: *The Definition of a Serious Security Library*

Syn•gress (sin–gres): *noun, sing.* Freedom from risk or danger; safety. See *security.*

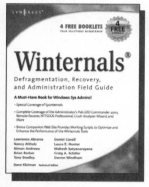

Winternals Defragmentation, Recovery, and Administration Field Guide

Dave Kleiman, Laura E. Hunter, Tony Bradley, Brian Barber, Nancy Altholz, Lawrence Abrams, Mahesh Satyanarayana, Darren Windham, Craig Schiller

As a system administrator for a Microsoft network, you know doubt spend too much of your life backing up data and restoring data, hunting down and removing malware and spyware, defragmenting disks, and improving the overall performance and reliability of your network. The Winternals® Defragmentation, Recovery, and Administration Field Guide and companion Web site provide you with all the information necessary to take full advantage of Winternals comprehensive and reliable tools suite for system administrators.

ISBN: 1-59749-079-2

Price: $49.95 US $64.95 CAN

Video Conferencing over IP: Configure, Secure, and Troubleshoot

Michael Gough

Until recently, the reality of videoconferencing didn't live up to the marketing hype. That's all changed. The network infrastructure and broadband capacity are now in place to deliver clear, real-time video and voice feeds between multiple points of contacts, with market leaders such as Cisco and Microsoft continuing to invest heavily in development. In addition, newcomers Skype and Google are poised to launch services and products targeting this market. *Video Conferencing over IP* is the perfect guide to getting up and running with video teleconferencing for small to medium-sized enterprises.

ISBN: 1-59749-063-6

Price: $49.95 U.S. $64.95 CAN

SYNGRESS®

Syngress: *The Definition of a Serious Security Library*

Syn·gress (sin–gres): *noun, sing.* Freedom from risk or danger; safety. See *security*.

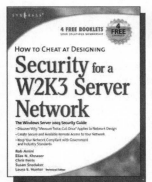

How to Cheat at Designing Security for a Windows Server 2003 Network

Neil Ruston, Chris Peiris

While considering the security needs of your organiztion, you need to balance the human and the technical in order to create the best security design for your organization. Securing a Windows Server 2003 enterprise network is hardly a small undertaking, but it becomes quite manageable if you approach it in an organized and systematic way. This includes configuring software, services, and protocols to meet an organization's security needs.

ISBN: 1-59749-243-4

Price: $39.95 US $55.95 CAN

How to Cheat at Designing a Windows Server 2003 Active Directory Infrastructure

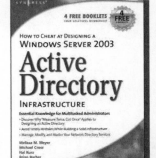

Melissa Craft, Michael Cross, Hal Kurz, Brian Barber

The book will start off by teaching readers to create the conceptual design of their Active Directory infrastructure by gathering and analyzing business and technical requirements. Next, readers will create the logical design for an Active Directory infrastructure. Here the book starts to drill deeper and focus on aspects such as group policy design. Finally, readers will learn to create the physical design for an active directory and network Infrastructure including DNS server placement; DC and GC placements and Flexible Single Master Operations (FSMO) role placement.

ISBN: 1-59749-058-X

Price: $39.95 US $55.95 CAN

How to Cheat at Configuring ISA Server 2004

Dr. Thomas W. Shinder, Debra Littlejohn Shinder

If deploying and managing ISA Server 2004 is just one of a hundred responsibilities you have as a System Administrator, "How to Cheat at Configuring ISA Server 2004" is the perfect book for you. Written by Microsoft MVP Dr. Tom Shinder, this is a concise, accurate, enterprise tested method for the successful deployment of ISA Server.

ISBN: 1-59749-057-1

Price: $34.95 U.S. $55.95 CAN

SYNGRESS®

Syngress: *The Definition of a Serious Security Library*

Syn•gress (sin–gres): *noun, sing.* Freedom from risk or danger; safety. See *security*.

Configuring SonicWALL Firewalls

Chris Lathem, Ben Fortenberry, Lars Hansen
Configuring SonicWALL Firewalls is the first book to deliver an in-depth look at the SonicWALL firewall product line. It covers all of the aspects of the SonicWALL product line from the SOHO devices to the Enterprise SonicWALL firewalls. Advanced troubleshooting techniques and the SonicWALL Security Manager are also covered.

ISBN: 1-59749-250-7
Price: $49.95 US $69.95 CAN

Perfect Passwords:
Selection, Protection, Authentication

Mark Burnett
User passwords are the keys to the network kingdom, yet most users choose overly simplistic passwords (like password) that anyone could guess, while system administrators demand impossible to remember passwords littered with obscure characters and random numerals. Author Mark Burnett has accumulated and analyzed over 1,000,000 user passwords, and this highly entertaining and informative book filled with dozens of illustrations reveals his findings and balances the rigid needs of security professionals against the ease of use desired by users.

ISBN: 1-59749-041-5
Price: $24.95 US $34.95 CAN

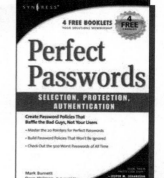

SYNGRESS®

Syngress: *The Definition of a Serious Security Library*

Syn·gress (sin–gres): *noun, sing.* Freedom from risk or danger; safety. See *security*.

Syngress: *The Definition of a Serious Security Library*

Syn•gress (sin–gres): *noun, sing.* Freedom from risk or danger; safety. See *security*.

How to Cheat at Managing Windows Server Update Services

Brian Barber

If you manage a Microsoft Windows network, you probably find yourself overwhelmed at times by the sheer volume of updates and patches released by Microsoft for its products. You know these updates are critical to keep your network running efficiently and securely, but staying current amidst all of your other responsibilities can be almost impossible. Microsoft's recently released Windows Server Update Services (WSUS) is designed to streamline this process. Learn how to take full advantage of WSUS using Syngress' proven "How to Cheat" methodology, which gives you everything you need and nothing you don't.

ISBN: 1-59749-027-X

Price: $39.95 US $55.95 CAN

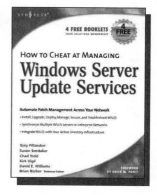

How to Cheat at IT Project Management

Susan Snedaker

Most IT projects fail to deliver – on average, all IT projects run over schedule by 82%, run over cost by 43% and deliver only 52% of the desired functionality. Pretty dismal statistics. Using the proven methods in this book, you'll find that IT project you work on from here on out will have a much higher likelihood of being on time, on budget and higher quality. This book provides clear, concise, information and hands-on training to give you immediate results. And, the companion Web site provides dozens of templates for managing IT projects.

ISBN: 1-59749-037-7

Price: $44.95 U.S. $64.95 CAN

SYNGRESS®

Syngress: *The Definition of a Serious Security Library*

Syn•gress (sin–gres): *noun, sing.* Freedom from risk or danger; safety. See *security*.

Managing Cisco Network Security, Second Edition

Offers updated and revised information covering many of Cisco's security products that provide protection from threats, detection of network security incidents, measurement of vulnerability and policy compliance, and management of security policy across an extended organization. These are the tools that you have to mount defenses against threats. Chapters also cover the improved functionality and ease of the Cisco Secure Policy Manager software used by thousands of small-to-midsized businesses, and a special section on Cisco wireless solutions.

ISBN: 1-931836-56-6

Price: $69.95 USA $108.95 CAN

How to Cheat at Managing Microsoft Operations Manager 2005

Tony Piltzecker, Rogier Dittner, Rory McCaw, Gordon McKenna, Paul M. Summitt, David E. Williams

My e-mail takes forever. My application is stuck. Why can't I log on? System administrators have to address these types of complaints far too often. With MOM, system administrators will know when overloaded processors, depleted memory, or failed network connections are affecting their Windows servers long before these problems bother users. Readers of this book will learn why when it comes to monitoring Windows Server System infrastructure, MOM's the word.

ISBN: 1-59749-251-5

Price: $39.95 U.S. $55.95 CAN

Syngress: *The Definition of a Serious Security Library*

Syn·gress (sin–gres): *noun, sing.* Freedom from risk or danger; safety. See *security*.

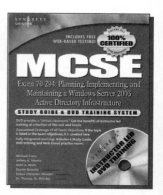

Syngress: *The Definition of a Serious Security Library*

Syn•gress (sin-gres): *noun, sing.* Freedom from risk or danger; safety. See *security*.

Syngress: *The Definition of a Serious Security Library*

Syn•gress (sin‑gres): *noun, sing.* Freedom from risk or danger; safety. See *security*.

Buffer OverFlow Attacks: Detect, Exploit, Prevent

James C. Foster, Foreword by Dave Aitel

The SANS Institute maintains a list of the "Top 10 Software Vulnerabilities." At the current time, over half of these vulnerabilities are exploitable by Buffer Overflow attacks, making this class of attack one of the most common and most dangerous weapons used by malicious attackers. This is the first book specifically aimed at detecting, exploiting, and preventing the most common and dangerous attacks.

ISBN: 1-932266-67-4

Price: $34.95 US $50.95 CAN

Programmer's Ultimate Security DeskRef

James C. Foster

The Programmer's Ultimate Security DeskRef is the only complete desk reference covering multiple languages and their inherent security issues. It will serve as the programming encyclopedia for almost every major language in use.

While there are many books starting to address the broad subject of security best practices within the software development lifecycle, none has yet to address the overarching technical problems of incorrect function usage. Most books fail to draw the line from covering best practices security principles to actual code implementation. This book bridges that gap and covers the most popular programming languages such as Java, Perl, C++, C#, and Visual Basic.

ISBN: 1-932266-72-0

Price: $49.95 US $72.95 CAN

Hacking the Code: ASP.NET Web Application Security

Mark Burnett

This unique book walks you through the many threats to your Web application code, from managing and authorizing users and encrypting private data to filtering user input and securing XML. For every defined threat, it provides a menu of solutions and coding considerations. And, it offers coding examples and a set of security policies for each of the corresponding threats.

ISBN: 1-932266-65-8

Price: $49.95 U.S. $79.95 CAN

SYNGRESS®

"Thieme's ability to be open minded, conspiratorial, ethical, and subversive all at the same time is very inspiring."*–Jeff Moss, CEO, Black Hat, Inc.*

Richard Thieme's Islands in the Clickstream: Reflections on Life in a Virtual World
Richard Thieme is one of the most visible commentators on technology and society, appearing regularly on CNN radio, TechTV, and various other national media outlets. He is also in great demand as a public speaker, delivering his "Human Dimension of Technology" talk to over 50,000 live audience members each year. *Islands in the Clickstream* is a single volume "best of Richard Thieme."
ISBN: 1-931836-22-1
Price: $29.95 US $43.95 CAN

"Thieme's Islands in the Clickstream is deeply reflective, enlightening, and refreshing." —*Peter Neumann, Stanford Research Institute*

"Richard Thieme takes us to the edge of cliffs we know are there but rarely visit ... he wonderfully weaves life, mystery, and passion through digital and natural worlds with creativity and imagination. This is delightful and deeply thought provoking reading full of "aha!" insights." —*Clinton C. Brooks, Senior Advisor for Homeland Security and Asst. Deputy Director, NSA*

"WOW! You eloquently express thoughts and ideas that I feel. You have helped me, not so much tear down barriers to communication, as to leverage these barriers into another structure with elevators and escalators."
—*Chip Meadows, CISSP, CCSE, USAA e-Security Team*

"Richard Thieme navigates the complex world of people and computers with amazing ease and grace. His clarity of thinking is refreshing, and his insights are profound." —*Bruce Schneier, CEO, Counterpane*

"I believe that you are a practioner of wu wei, the effort to choose the elegant appropriate contribution to each and every issue that you address." —*Hal McConnell (fomer intelligence analyst, NSA)*

"Richard Thieme presents us with a rare gift. His words touch our heart while challenging our most cherished constructs. He is both a poet and pragmatist navigating a new world with clarity, curiosity and boundless amazement." —*Kelly Hansen, CEO, Neohapsis*

"Richard Thieme combines hi-tech, business savvy and social consciousness to create some of the most penetrating commentaries of our times. A column I am always eager to read." —*Peter Russell, author "From Science to God"*

"These reflections provide a veritable feast for the imagination, allowing us more fully to participate in Wonder. This book is an experience of loving Creation with our minds." —*Louie Crew, Member of Executive Council of The Episcopal Church*

"The particular connections Richard Thieme makes between mind, heart, technology, and truth, lend us timely and useful insight on what it means to live in a technological era. Richard fills a unique and important niche in hacker society!" —*Mick Bauer, Security Editor, Linux Journal*

SYNGRESS®